PUB W
IN
North London

G000113794

Other areas covered in the Pub Walks series include:

Bedfordshire
Berkshire
Birmingham & Coventry
Bournemouth & Poole
Bristol & Bath
Buckinghamshire
Cambridgeshire
Cheshire
Chilterns
Cotswolds
Cotswold Way
County Durham
North & West Cumbria
South Cumbria
Dartmoor & South Devon
Derbyshire
Essex
West Essex
Exmoor & North Devon
Gloucestershire
Herefordshire
Hertfordshire
Icknield Way Path
Isle of Wight
Kent – the North Downs
Lancashire

Leicestershire & Rutland
Lincolnshire
Middlesex & West London
Midshires Way
Norfolk
Northamptonshire
Nottinghamshire
Oxfordshire
Shropshire
South Downs
Staffordshire
Suffolk
Surrey
Surrey Hills
Thames Valley
North Wales
South Wales
Warwickshire
Wayfarer's Walk
Wiltshire
Worcestershire
Wye Valley & Forest of Dean
East Yorkshire
North Yorkshire
South Yorkshire
West Yorkshire

A complete catalogue is available from the publisher at
3 Catherine Road, Newbury, Berkshire

P U B   W A L K S

IN

North London

TWENTY CIRCULAR WALKS
AROUND NORTH LONDON INNS

Leigh Hatts

COUNTRYSIDE BOOKS
NEWBURY, BERKSHIRE

COUNTRYSIDE BOOKS
3 Catherine Road
Newbury, Berkshire

ISBN 1 85306 427 0

Designed by Mon Mohan
Cover illustration by Colin Doggett
Photographs by the author
Maps by Jack Street

Produced through MRM Associates Ltd., Reading
Printed by Woolnough Bookbinding, Irthlingborough

Contents

Publisher's Note

We hope that you obtain considerable enjoyment from this book; great care has been taken in its preparation. However, changes of landlord and actual closures are sadly not uncommon. Likewise, although at the time of publication all routes followed public rights of way or permitted paths, diversion orders can be made and permissions withdrawn.

We cannot of course be held responsible for such diversion orders and any inaccuracies in the text which result from these or any other changes to the routes nor any damage which might result from walkers trespassing on private property. We are anxious though that all details covering the walks and the pubs are kept up to date and would therefore welcome information from readers which would be relevant to future editions.

Area map showing locations of the walks.

Introduction

North London pubs have experienced great change in the last decade. The changes are not all bad for there has been a return to old values.

London pubs, like those in the Home Counties, have greatly increased the range of food on offer and the warmth of welcome to the visitor. Some inns closed down during the recession but many which survived appear alert to the needs of the traveller. This is in the tradition of the inn, which in the past always offered the best food in the town or village.

Many of the pubs in this book are in London's villages. Some are famous and often busy such as the Flask at Highgate and others are tiny and quiet like the Woodman at Southgate. That is as it should be. The Flask was once always full of drovers whilst the Woodman was just a cottage selling beer. Another return to the values of the past is the widespread availability and wide choice of real ales.

The biggest change has been in the laws allowing all day opening and Sunday afternoon opening. This is not welcomed by all landlords and some pubs are not taking advantage yet of the easier laws. Indeed, some which opened on Sunday afternoons as soon as the law allowed have found themselves without customers even on hot days and have already reverted to the old hours. But sometimes the longer afternoon opening has meant that lunchtime is less crowded. This is still early days but the reader must be ready for an unexpected afternoon closure or opening.

There is even a new major landmark which can be seen on many of the walks including the most northerly and certainly those with viewpoints. This is Canary Wharf on the Isle of Dogs. Originally just a wharf where cargo from the Canaries was unloaded, now the Docklands' site is occupied by the 50 floor, 850 ft tower which appeared on the skyline towards the end of the Eighties. It is Britain's tallest building and, since being occupied in 1991, is now claimed as Europe's highest office block. The tower, designed to sway over a foot in a high wind, is home to several immigrants from Fleet Street including *The Daily Telegraph*, *The Daily Mirror* and *The Independent*.

Another familiar feature on these walks will be the New River, which flows near three of the pubs – in one case past the front door. This is an artificial waterway dug between 1608 and 1613 under a plan masterminded by Hugh Myddleton, who faced opposition from landowners who feared that the 10 ft wide channel would be a danger to men and cattle. However, Myddleton, who was jeweller to the king, won James I's support and financial backing for the scheme to bring fresh drinking water from Hertfordshire to central London. Although the water was collected from the river Lea just 20 miles away the New River took 38 miles to reach the capital. Today the tortuous loops are a delightful green corridor for walkers.

If you are leaving your car in a pub car park it is advisable to check with the landlord before setting out – normally there will not be any problems.

But London has special problems. It is not just the central London pubs which lack parking spaces and often the car is not the best option. All the walks in this book can easily be reached by public transport. Indeed, a one day Travel Card allows unlimited travel within Greater London on bus, Underground and British Rail. On a summer day you might manage two pub visits on one day on one ticket.

Each walk carries details of the Ordnance Survey maps covering the area. However, in London, it is obviously sensible to use a street map – A4 size spiral bound London street maps are published by Nicholson and Geographia. These handy sized books do not cover the Enfield town walk or the circuit from Bulls Cross taking in Temple Bar but these two walks will be found in the local Enfield map and the A-Z Master Atlas of Greater London – although the Bulls Cross walk can easily be followed on the OS Pathfinder maps indicated.

London has plenty of pubs as good and unusual as those in the country. Indeed, many are found in London's rural corners, easily reached by public transport from the city centre. I hope that now the pub visit can be an opportunity to visit those historic, hidden corners of London you have always intended exploring.

I am grateful to Rosemary Clarke and James Hatts for their advice and help.

Leigh Hatts
Spring 1996

① Old Redding, Harrow Weald
The Case is Altered

The Case is Altered displays a sign showing British troops at a Spanish inn on top of a high hill so the name could be a corruption of 'La Casa Alta' meaning 'high house'. This London pub is on top of a hill with a view of five counties. However, it is also sometimes called 'The Cathedral' and another explanation for the name is that as a Father Casey said mass in the pub during times of persecution it was known as 'Casey's Altar'. Locally it is held that the brickmakers in this area went to law to determine who owned this high point.

The small building is at least 200 years old, and the garden has a large sloping lawn with plenty of tables and a children's area complete with swings, slides and a see-saw all on a soft surface. Food can be taken outside – indeed there is often a barbecue on the terrace.

The main menu chalked up inside features roast beef, tuna and ham rolls; a Brie, Stilton or Cheddar ploughman's; salads; Hawaiian and vegetarian burgers with fries. Side orders include garlic bread.

Among the main courses are Tetley beef pie and a selection of puddings such as home-made trifle and chocolate fudge cake. There are always five real ales available including a guest ale – regulars are Tetley, Burton and local Watford Benskins.

The Case is Altered is open all day 11 am to 11 pm. The Sunday hours are 12 noon to 10.30 pm. Food is available at least between 12 noon and 2.30 pm.

Telephone: 0181 954 1002.

How to get there: The Case is Altered is in Old Redding which runs between the A4008 Oxhey Lane and the A409 Brookshill at Harrow Weald near Stanmore. Buses 258 and 350 (not Sundays) run from Harrow-on-the-Hill station to pass the east end of Old Redding.

Parking: There is parking at the viewpoint on the west side of the pub.

Length of the walk: 3 miles. Map: A-Z London Street Map; OS Pathfinder 1139 Watford & Rickmansworth; OS Landranger 176 West London (inn GR 144926).

This walk starts by a viewpoint and circles estate land where the walker will find not only farm buildings but may encounter Highland cattle and deer. Bentley Priory, named after a dissolved religious house, is a former royal residence which became the operations centre for the RAF during the Battle of Britain.

The Walk
Leave the pub and turn right and right again into a gravelled track signed Suzanne's Riding School. The way bends by Copse Farm. Keep left at a divide and go left again up a track where a signpost points to Brookshill. Go past the riding school as the path climbs to the main road at the far end. Turn right for a short distance before going left down a path marked Clamp Hill.

At first the sheltered path is on a wooded ledge and later emerges at a road. Cross over to the pavement and go right. Just before the road bears round to the left go sharp left down the entrance to Lower Priory Farm. Follow the wooded track and at a gateway go to the right to find a kissing-gate. The sheltered path ahead follows

11

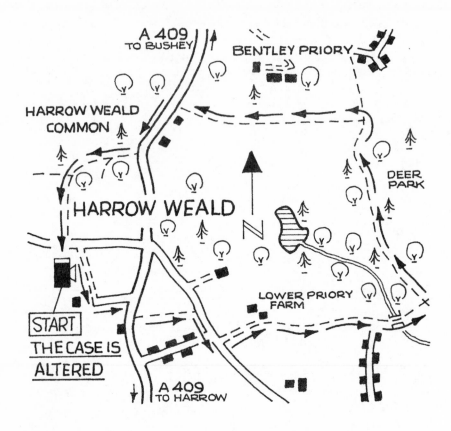

a drainage ditch along the bottom of Bentley Priory grounds. Soon after passing some houses at the end of a road the path bears half left to cross a footbridge. Beyond the kissing-gate the path runs through a wood to emerge on open grassland – there may be cattle grazing here.

The path can be seen running ahead across the grass towards a signpost. (One of the four signs points to Stanmore church which is really two churches – the ruin and the Victorian successor side by side. W.S. Gilbert of Gilbert and Sullivan is buried in the churchyard.) The walk continues to the left following the sign pointing to Stanmore Common. This is a more substantial path with a metalled surface which, beyond a kissing-gate, enters a wood. Later there is a fenced deer park to the right.

On emerging from the trees there is a glimpse half left of the Bentley Priory clock tower. At a signpost go left towards Harrow Weald Common. The path is a narrow concrete one with the high fence of Bentley Priory to the right. The priory founded in 1170 was to the south and only moved up the hill as a secular residence in 1775. This was the home of William IV's widow, Queen Adelaide who died here in 1849. It later became a hotel and was purchased by the Air Ministry in 1925. It was from this high vantage point that Lord Dowding directed the Battle of Britain in 1940. Stay on the path as it winds, falls and rises. Later there is a fine view over to the left, just before the path meets a kissing-gate.

The path is through a tunnel of rhododendrons to a large gate by a road. Cross over to a pavement and go left.

Just past Princess Alexandra Home and near the road bend go right between the white posts to follow a wide woodland path. Stay on this path as it narrows, ignoring a branch to the left, to reach two white posts at a T-junction, almost opposite the North Lodge gateway of Grims Dyke House, once home of W.S. Gilbert. The walk continues to the left up the straight path. At a gateway leading onto a road go right to find the Case is Altered.

2 Mill Hill
The Three Hammers

At the top of steep Hammers Lane are three of Mill Hill's noted buildings. Murray House is where Sir James Murray began work on the *Oxford English Dictionary* in 1870, the attractive butcher's is well known for its home-made sausages and the Three Hammers has a sign showing the blacksmith at work when the village was on the London road.

The exterior of the Three Hammers is not as attractive as the cottages opposite but the inside of the brick pub building is a surprise with real books on the bookshelves and historic photographs on the walls. By the food counter there is a reproduction of James O'Connor's 1884 painting *St Pancras Hotel and Station from Pentonville Road* showing St James's Pentonville, visited on the Waterside at King's Cross walk (see Walk 17). Food can be eaten in a family dining area in the conservatory, or in the garden.

The cold menu includes baguettes filled with tuna and mayonnaise, beef and horseradish or cheese and pickle. Similar toppings are available for jacket potatoes. Among the main dishes

No 3 Church Cottages has an unusual garden path.

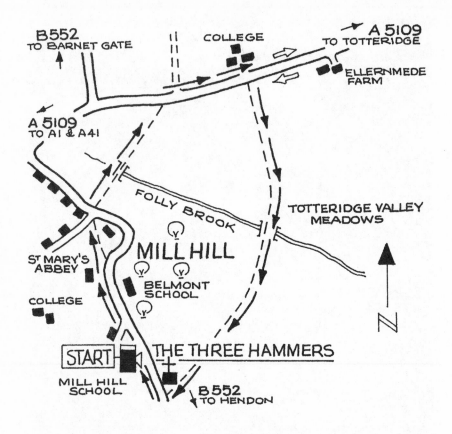

are steak and kidney pie and cod and prawn crumble. There are always at least three vegetarian dishes including Venetian pasta boats – pasta filled with sweetcorn, celery, mushrooms and peppers in a cheese and tomato sauce. There is also a children's menu and such puddings as Banana Bash for all ages.

This is a Taylor Walker house serving Taylor Walker Best Bitter, Ind Coope's Burton Ale and Tetley Bitter. The opening hours are 11 am to 3 pm and 5.30 pm to 11 pm with food served at lunchtime and from 7 pm to 9 pm in the evening. The Sunday hours are 12 noon to 10.30 pm with food available until 4 pm and from 7 pm to 9 pm.

Telephone: 0181 959 2346.

16

How to get there: Mill Hill is on the B552 which runs between Highwood Hill and Holders Hill. The Three Hammers is at the junction with the B1461 at the western end of The Ridgeway, NW7. Bus 240 runs between Mill Hill Broadway BR station and Mill Hill East Underground station and stops outside the Three Hammers.

Parking: There is a car park at the pub.

Length of the walk: 2 miles. Map: A-Z London Street Map; OS Pathfinder 1140 Barnet and Enfield; OS Landranger 176 West London (inn GR 224928).

Mill Hill retains its village charm which attracted so many leading Londoners to have a home here in the 18th and 19th centuries. The route is across the Totteridge Valley meadows which could be far from the capital. A short diversion will find a farm selling milk and cream produced on site.

The Walk
Leave the corner pub and cross over the top of Hammers Lane with the butcher's to the left. From this T-junction continue west along The Ridgeway passing The Old Mill House on the site of the hilltop mill which gave Mill Hill its name. On the far side of the road is Belmont School, former home of two Lord Mayors of London including John Wilkes who became Lord Mayor in 1774. Soon to the left there is a view over Mill Field towards St Joseph's College, built in 1871 as the mother house of the missionaries, the Mill Hill Fathers, known as the MHF. A little further on is Holcombe House, another Lord Mayor's house, where the future Cardinal Vaughan began his order in 1866.

Continue past St Mary's Abbey and ahead down the steep footpath to a road junction by a bus stop. Turn right to pass the Old Forge which was operating until 1932. Cross the road to a kissing-gate and once in the field bear half right. The footbridge will be handy if there is water in the ditch as you approach a stile by a barrier. Beyond here the way is half left across the centre of the field to the far corner – the track sometimes runs up by the hedge for a few yards before the hay is cut in June.

In the far corner cross the stiles and Folly Brook footbridge and continue ahead. There is another stile in a fence before the path

The village sign.

continues ahead up the side of the valley. At the top bear round to the right to find a fine white wooden farm and kissing-gates.

Continue forward along the side of the road. There is a wide verge but the footpath is to be found on the left side set back from the road. Continue as far as the post box outside St Andrew's College on the left.

Here the walk leaves the road but those wishing to visit Ellern Mede Farm to buy local milk, cream, honey or eggs should continue ahead to the next bus stop 300 yards further on. Ellern Mede was designed by Norman Shaw and built in 1876. The farm shop is open 9 am to 5.30 pm except Sunday afternoon.

At the post box at St Andrew's College turn right to cross the road and go down a rough path. As it swings right keep forward to a stile to follow the straight sheltered path which runs down into the valley. After the Folly Brook footbridge the path climbs up to Mill Hill with a view of the Medical Research Institute over to the south-east. Beyond a wood the path follows the side of a playground up to a kissing-gate leading to The Ridgeway.

Opposite is Mill Hill School, founded in 1807, where recent pupils have included Sir Norman Hartnell and Sir Denis Thatcher. Turn right to pass the smaller village school and St Paul's church, built by the reformer William Wilberforce in 1829 to the annoyance of the nearby vicar of Hendon whose private income was derived from slave plantations. Next door are Church Cottages where number 3 has a path laid in the 1860s using upturned ink pots from Mill Hill School. Continue past Sheepwash Pond where sheep were washed on their way to Smithfield's live meat market. On the left is the Three Hammers.

Totteridge
The Orange Tree

The Orange Tree is found in a corner of Totteridge Green with a pond and willow trees opposite the front door. Inside there is a horseshoe-shaped bar and the two rooms have plenty of corners to sit including in the window. Some of the pictures show Totteridge in past times but the big colourful painting is an original of the pub today by local artist Liz Armstrong. In summer many customers drink and eat outdoors by the water or on the grass at the side.

This is a Toby house so as well as sandwiches at the bar there is an extensive menu in the separate restaurant area, offering mixed grill, steak pie, bacon wrapped chicken breast, steaks and fish including seafood salad. Vegetarian dishes include cream Brie and courgette crumble, mushroom strudel and cashew nut paella. Among the regular puddings included in the main course price are two fruit cheesecake, banana and toffee pie and old-fashioned sherry trifle. Also available are children's meals. The popular lunchtime food in the bar is the baguette – three small sized ones – filled with such combinations as tuna and mayonnaise, ham and mustard or cheese and pickle and served with salad.

As a Toby inn the ales include draught Bass as well as Worthington Best Bitter, Charrington IPA and Fuller's London Pride. The Orange Tree is open from 11 am to 3 pm and 5.30 pm to 11 pm. At weekends there is no afternoon closure. On Sunday the hours are 12 noon to 10.30 pm. The restaurant is open 12 noon to 2 pm and 6 pm to 10 pm and all day on Sunday.

Telephone: 0181 445 6542.

How to get there: Totteridge is on the A5109 between Whetstone and Edgware. Bus 251 runs through the village from Totteridge & Whetstone Underground station. The Orange Tree is by Totteridge Green, N20.

Parking: There is a car park at the pub.

Length of the walk: 3 miles. Map: A-Z London Street Map; OS Pathfinder 1140 Barnet & Enfield; OS Landranger 176 West London (inn GR 249938).

Totteridge has been described as having 'the finest example of traditional English countryside in the London area' and the rural landscape is defended from encroachment by a vigilant Barnet Council which also maintains its footpath network well. This route makes use of those paths to view the countryside where the nearest milking herd to central London grazes. There is even a farm shop.

The Walk
Turn left out of the pub to reach the main road, known simply as Totteridge Village, and go left to walk up to the church. The pavement on the right-hand side may be more pleasant – and handy if visiting the church. Totteridge church is unusual for being in north-west London but coming under the jurisdiction of St Albans Diocese. This is because Totteridge was never part of Middlesex and until 1965 was a Hertfordshire village. The Georgian church was built in 1790 but the weather-boarded bell turret dates from at least 1706. At the time of the Battle of Waterloo the congregation included the future Cardinal Manning whose father and brother are buried in the churchyard – under the holly tree by the north-east corner of the church. (Golfer Harry Vardon is buried in the churchyard extension – on the right after the path turns right.) The

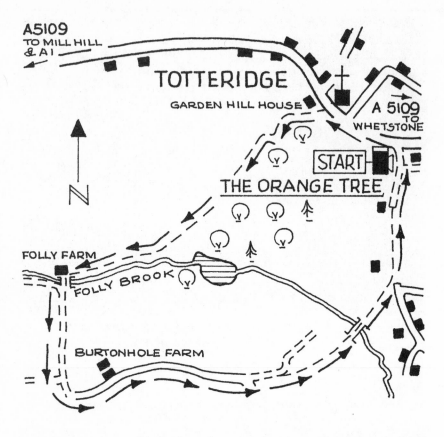

great yew tree was here when the previous church was on the site. Just outside the lychgate and behind a hedge is the village cattle pound.

Opposite the church is Garden Hill House, home of Lord Chief Justice Hewart in the inter-war years. Go through the gateway to the left of the house. The enclosed path soon runs downhill on the edge of a wood with views north over rolling countryside. At the bottom of the hill the path runs straight for ¾ mile to a stile. Ahead on a hill is the huge National Institute for Medical Research building completed in 1939. Go half left over the field towards the landmark building. On the far side do not go through the gate but over the stile. Ignore the turning right to Long Ponds and follow the path ahead running alongside Folly Brook.

Totteridge church.

At the gateway to the modern Folly Farm turn left to walk alongside a cricket ground with the view dominated again by the research building. After a garden centre the lane bears left to a junction. Turn left along Burtonhole Lane. Soon there is Burtonhole Farm on the left where milk, cream, eggs and jam can be purchased between 9.30 am and 3.30 pm daily except Mondays.

Soon the metalled road becomes a rough bridleway. After just over ¼ mile look out for a squeeze stile by a gate on a double bend. A signpost says 'Totteridge ¾'. Go through the stile and ahead along the side of a field. At the next field the way bears left uphill with views to the right over to houses in Woodside Park. The path then drops down to a stile at a barrier. Continue uphill. There is another stile by a gate before reaching a stile at the top of the hill. Here the way is enclosed, with a second stile to dissuade horses, before the path reaches the pond at the south end of Totteridge Green.

Turn left to walk up to the main road. The Orange Tree is to the left by another pond.

4 Barnet
The Green Man

Barnet's full name is Chipping Barnet and 'chipping' means 'market', which is held on Wednesdays and Saturdays near the Green Man. Even the annual Barnet Horse Fair still takes place every September. Barnet is set on high ground 10 miles from central London with the keyhole of St John's church on a level with the top of the cross on St Paul's Cathedral dome. Most pubs here were coaching inns providing the last change of horses before London. The modern glass-fronted Green Man, renovated in 1991, does not look old but there has been a Green Man on the site for over 150 years. It lost part of its yard and became a corner pub in 1828 when St Albans Road was built as part of Thomas Telford's new road to Holyhead. Sir Robert Peel and Lord Palmerston both stayed here – this was a Whig inn with the Tories patronising the Red Lion.

The upstairs pool room is known as the Warwick Room after Warwick the Kingmaker who was defeated at the Battle of Barnet in the Wars of the Roses. But the bar is downstairs in the wood panelled lounge decorated with pictures of ships. There is a juke box and a television which are sometimes on at the same time when early Saturday sport is being shown.

There are always ploughman's and sandwiches. Beef and chicken burgers are served with salad and chips. Specials can include ham salad, turkey salad, lasagne salad and chicken tikka. Children are welcome at lunchtime, especially for traditional lunch on Sunday, but not in the evenings. This is a town pub but it is also a McMullen of Hertford house so it's well supplied with the much praised local Gladstone Bitter along with Original AK.

The opening hours are 11 am to 3 pm and 5.30 pm to 11 pm. On Sunday the opening hours are 12 noon to 3 pm and 7 pm to 10.30 pm.
Telephone: 0181 449 4033.

How to get there: Barnet is north of Finchley and on the A1000. High Barnet station is the end of the Northern Line. The Green Man is on the corner of Barnet High Street and St Albans Road.

Parking: There is no parking at the pub, but there is a Pay & Display car park in nearby Stapylton Road.

Length of the walk: 2½ miles. Map: A-Z London Street Map; OS Pathfinder 1140 Barnet & Enfield; OS Landranger 176 West London (inn GR 245968).

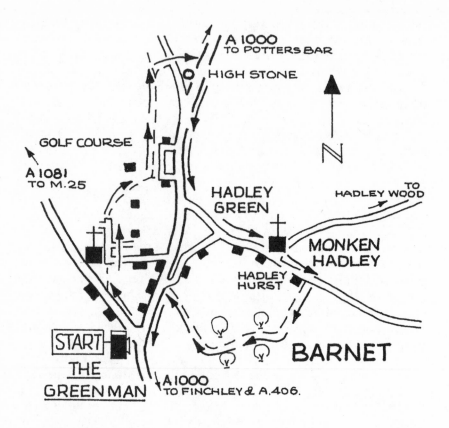

The walk circles Hadley Green where the Wars of the Roses came to an end with the Battle of Barnet on Easter Day 1471 when Edward IV and his army, marching from London, defeated the Earl of Warwick, who was slain. Hadley means 'high' and the green is bisected by the Great North Road which here is at its highest point between London and York. The church still has a beacon attached to the tower.

The Walk
Turn left out of the Green Man and go up St Albans Road to pass the market ground. It is best to walk on the right-hand side. On coming level with number 41 turn right up a narrow passage – a notice forbids horse riding. Later the way, known as Christ Church

Passage, crosses Hadley Grove where there is a view back to Christ Church, built in 1845 on Four Acre Field which until then was rented by the landlord of the Green Man.

After passing Sunset View the path narrows again to run along the edge of a golf course. At the far end the path bears right to Hadley Green. Here turn left to pass a pond and Old Fold Manor. Keep ahead past the golf club, a much restored farmhouse, and a terrace of houses. At End Cottage the way becomes rough. The path follows the Greater London boundary – Hertfordshire to the left and London to the right – although until 1965 Hadley Green was part of Hertfordshire. Where the way bears right to a fork, keep right to reach the road at Hadley High Stone.

Turn right down Kitts End Road to the High Stone. Here the road divides to run each side of Wrotham Park, the Byng family estate. The 80 room mansion was completed in 1754 for Admiral Byng who three years later was executed for failing to relieve Minorca during the Seven Years' War. More recently in 1995 it was the venue for Greek Prince Pavlos' pre-wedding ball attended by several crowned heads. In 1471 Warwick the Kingmaker came down Kitts End Lane for the battle which the High Stone commemorates.

The Edwardian style houses along the Great North Road were built in 1995 to replace the Two Brewers. Continue along the main road past charming small cottages to find two remaining pubs – the 17th-century William IV freehouse alongside the old school and the Old Windmill. Continue ahead to go left into Dury Road. Soon the houses on the right give way to the Green where there are two ponds. At a junction by St Martha's Convent keep forward past the end of the 1612 Wilbraham Almshouses to reach Monken Hadley church.

The church was built in 1494 just over 20 years after the battle. 'Monken' recalls that the church belonged to Malden Abbey in Essex. The beacon on the tower, dating from the time of the Spanish Armada threat when there was a nationwide chain, is lit on very special occasions such as the 50th VE anniversary. The church is featured in *The Bertrams* by Anthony Trollope, whose sister is buried in the churchyard.

Go through the gateway on to Hadley Common which is part of the Enfield Chase hunting ground where highwayman Dick Turpin operated. Continue ahead, ignoring Camlet Way to pass the pond opposite the 18th-century Gladsmuir, known as The Lemmons when it was the home of Kingsley Amis and Elizabeth Jane Howard who both feature it in their novels – *Girl 20* and *Odd Girl Out*. In 1972 Poet Laureate C. Day Lewis died here shortly after writing his last poem called *At Lemmons*. Further along is Hadley Hurst which was designed by Sir Christopher Wren and this century has been the home of shipping magnate Sir Ernest Glover and the 2nd Lord Netherthorpe.

Just past the Hadley Hurst gateway turn right through a small gateway flanked by a lion and a unicorn. The path leads to King George's playing field. On reaching the sweep of grass leave the path by going right and right again. Here can be seen the Alexandra Palace mast and the BT tower. Stay on the main rough path ahead to go through the band of trees. Once in the open take the right fork to walk downhill. At the bottom there may be some water. Once up the steep wooded bank keep forward across grass to meet a firm wide path at a T-junction. Turn right to go uphill through a gap. Keep forward with Barnet's St John's church seen over to the left. Near the top look back to see Canary Wharf tower in Docklands. Here at the top of the hill was the right flank of Edward IV's army during the Battle of Barnet.

Go over the stile and take the left fork to find a kissing-gate at Hadley Green. Across the road there is a pond. Turn left to reach Barnet High Street and the Green Man.

5 Hampstead Heath
The Spaniards

The Spaniards, an early 17th-century building, may have been the home of the Spanish ambassador during James I's reign although another suggestion for the name is that two Spanish brothers were once the landlords. A later landlord in 1780 had the presence of mind to ply the Gordon Rioters with enough drink to make them incapable of going on to burn down Kenwood House, home of the Lord Chief Justice. Soldiers sent from London found them slumped on the floor. In May 1819 artist Joseph Severn found the poet Keats lying in the garden listening to a nightingale just a few days before he produced his *Ode to a Nightingale*.

Now there are exotic birds in a cage at the bottom of the garden. Charles Dickens knew the pub and in *Pickwick Papers* he has Mrs Bardel arrested here. Opposite is a tollhouse where Dick Turpin stabled Black Bess. Although the highwayman is said to have hidden at the pub when evading the law it is the horse rather than Turpin who is reported to haunt the Spaniards with hoofbeats heard at night.

There are several tiny rooms with low ceilings and one is devoted

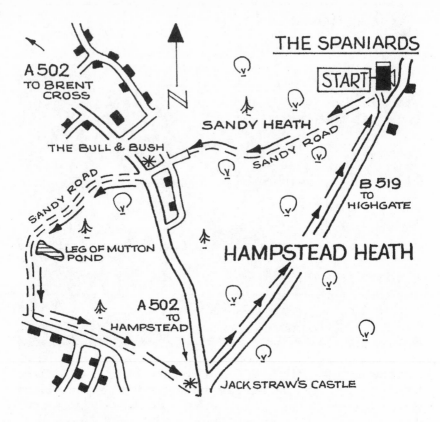

to food. The menu changes daily and the lunch menu is not the same as the evening menu. However, there is usually a choice of ploughman's from Cheddar, pâté, mackerel and smoked salmon. Specials include vegetable moussaka and vegetable curry. Apple and sultana sponge pudding is sometimes included on the board above the counter. Cappuccino and hot chocolate are available. This is a Charrington house, with Draught Bass, Worthington Best Bitter, Hancock's and Fuller's London Pride.

The Spaniards has the Camden-Barnet borough boundary running through the building which led to one part of the house having different licensing hours from the other. Today the entire pub is open from 11 am to 11 pm with food available from noon to 3 pm and 6 pm to 9.30 pm. On Saturdays there is food all afternoon. Sunday opening times are 12 noon to 10.30 pm.

Telephone: 0181 455 3276.

How to get there: The Spaniards is on the B519 at the point where Spaniards Road, NW3 meets Hampstead Lane on the north side of Hampstead Heath. Bus 240 runs between Archway and Hampstead Underground stations and stops outside.

Parking: There is a car park at the inn.

Length of the walk: 2 miles. Map: OS Pathfinder 1159 City of London; OS Landranger 176 West London (inn GR 267873).

This walk explores the north-west corner of Hampstead Heath near Golders Green and Childs Hill where the Heath is mainly woodland. On the way there is another famous pub in an attractive setting.

The Walk
Turn right out of the pub to be on the Hampstead side of the toll gate. After a short distance there is Evergreen Hill which has a blue plaque to Dame Henrietta Barnett, founder of Hampstead Garden Suburb, and her husband Canon Barnett who saved Sandy Heath from being built over for a North End station on the Northern Line. The wife of American artist James Whistler died here whilst the couple were renting the house in 1895. Cross the small entrance to Spaniards End and leave the main road to go past a barrier and into the Sandy Heath woodland.

Follow the main path ahead which is known as Sandy Road. The trees blot out the traffic noise. Later there is a small pond. At the second and larger pond the path does a double bend downhill to become a metalled road at North End. Keep ahead over a crossroads to pass the attractive Wildwood Lodge.

At the main road turn right to find the Bull and Bush pub. The 'Bull' recalls that this site was a farmhouse, once the country home of artist William Hogarth who planted yew trees – hence the 'Bush'. But the overall theme is of music hall star Florrie Forde who sang the famous song *Down at the old Bull and Bush* said to have been written here. Part of the building is much older than it at first looks.

Use the crossing to reach Sandy Road opposite. Go up the road

31

which bears right to a barrier. Continue on the rough surface. There are trees to the left and on the right views over Golders Hill Park which was saved for the public in 1898 by Pears Soap chairman, Thomas Barratt. Mill Hill is in the distance. The path runs south-west to turn south at Leg of Mutton Pond.

The name is said not to come from its shape but from an experiment by a Hampstead resident who was so sure of the water's purity that he threw a leg of mutton into the pond on a warm day and later enjoyed the meat without any ill effects. In the 1830s it was popular with washer women but today it is home to moorhens, mallards and tufted ducks.

Continue ahead to reach West Heath Road. Turn left to follow the path along the side of the road. Opposite is a line of large houses including a vast baronial Tudor style residence. As the road swings to the right keep forward on the worn path . There is meadowland to the left before the way begins to climb and later becomes stepped. At the top of the hill is the Whitestone Pond road junction.

The pond, which takes its name from a milestone, is to the right and in the early morning the King's Troop sometimes rides through the water during an outing from its St John's Wood stables. The radio mast is on the site of the beacon which warned of the Spanish Armada.

Turn left for a few yards to cross the road on the crossing. On the far side go left to walk up Spaniards Road. Immediately on the left, at the road fork, is Heath House where banker Samuel Hoare entertained poet William Wordsworth and reformer William Wilberforce.

Keep ahead up Spaniards Road, with the Heath on both sides, to reach the Spaniards.

6 Hampstead
The Freemasons Arms

Downshire Hill is one of the most attractive streets in the hilltop village of Hampstead. Approached from the High Street and Rosslyn Hill, the main shopping area, you have a view of the very attractive private chapel of St John which stands at the junction with Keats Grove. Keats saw this church, with its charming porch and cupola, being built and Byron was a friend of the first chaplain. George Bernard Shaw, D.H. Lawrence, Stanley Spencer, Katharine Mansfield, Flora Robson and Edith Sitwell are just some of the names who have been associated with this largely Regency road.

The last building on the left is the Freemasons Arms which at first looks quite out of place. There has been a pub on the site since at least 1819 but, unlike the houses, it was rebuilt in the early 1930s. However, its position is handy for the Heath opposite and the great attraction in summer is the garden. In the basement there is a skittle alley claimed by some to be England's last pell mell ground – the once popular game was played in St James's, hence Pall Mall – and by others to be simply London skittles. Upstairs there are playing cards, dominoes and shove halfpenny.

The inside of the pub is traditional and, with the open fire and a room suitable for families, a little like a hotel. The menu, chalked up on a board, usually has soup, ploughman's and steak and kidney pie. In summer there is direct service for outdoor diners. This is a Charrington house with Adnams Bitter, Draught Bass, Hancock's HB and Fuller's London Pride.

The Freemasons Arms is open 11 am to 11 pm with food available from 12 noon to 10 pm. The Sunday opening hours are 12 noon to 10.30 pm.

Telephone: 0171 435 4498.

How to get there: Hampstead's Rosslyn Hill is on the A502 just north of Camden Town. Downshire Hill NW3 is a turning on the north side. The nearest Underground station is Hampstead. Also nearby is Hampstead Heath BR station.

Parking: There is a public car park opposite on the Heath.

Length of the walk: 2½ miles. Map: A-Z London Street Map; OS Pathfinder 1159 City of London; OS Landranger 176 West London (inn GR 271859).

Hampstead Heath, London's highest open space, is 768 acres of countryside saved in 1871 and now trapped inside Greater London. However, the surrounding suburbia is often hidden from view and in the Second World War a pilot who made a forced landing was amazed to find himself just 5 miles from Charing Cross. Here can be found at least 200 varieties of flowering plants and such wildlife as voles, water rats, weasels and snakes. Woodpeckers are among the birdlife. This route circles the main part of the Heath taking in a most rewarding viewpoint, the ponds and an historic corner of the village on the way back.

The Walk

Turn left out of the pub forecourt to go over the crossroads and the East Heath Road main road. Keep forward on the wide path at the side of the car park on the left. Ahead are the Hampstead Ponds.

Do not continue ahead between the ponds but bear left. Stay on this main path as it swings right to pass between the two upper ponds. There may be bathers in the left-hand pond. On the far side

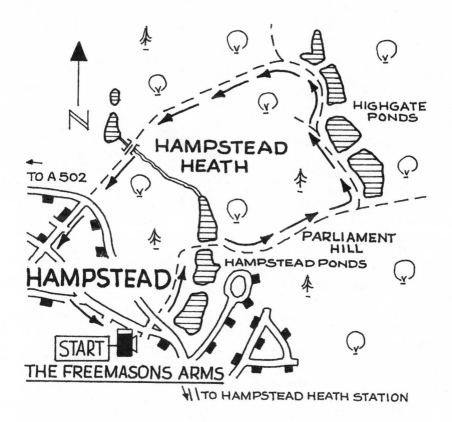

follow the main path round to the right and at a junction take the right-hand metalled path. Stay on this path which runs near the backs of waterside houses and over two path junctions as it climbs Parliament Hill. The name is said to recall the Gunpowder Plotters' plan to watch the destruction of the Palace of Westminster from this 320 ft high vantage point in November 1605.

Half left there is a view of Highgate with St Michael's spire on the hilltop and on the southern slope there is the green dome of St Joseph's dating from 1888 and known locally as 'Holy Joe's'. Half right is Canary Wharf tower on the Isle of Dogs seen in front of Shooters Hill. Walking ahead downhill there is the London panorama over to the right.

Keep forward at a minor junction but at the major junction take the left fork to continue down to the Highgate Ponds. Ahead on the way is the stone steeple of St Anne's Brookfield built in 1855. At the bottom go left to pass the chain of Highgate Ponds created in the 17th century to provide water for London. At the end of the second pond bear half right at the junction past the Boating Pond on the right.

At the end of this pond bear left. The next pond, on the right, is fenced as it is a bird sanctuary. The path now becomes rough as it begins to run very gently uphill. Where the way divides keep left. The ground continues to gently climb. Still keep on this main path which after a junction begins to run downhill between lime trees. After crossing the infant river Fleet, which later flows beneath Holborn Viaduct and Farringdon Street, the way climbs again. This is known as Boundary Path – look for the LCC boundary stone by the flats on the left just before the road.

Cross East Heath Road to Well Walk. There is a seat on the corner where Keats used to sit looking at the Heath. Keep on the high pavement on the right to pass the site of the Hampstead Wells which made Hampstead famous in the early 18th century. The first of many literary figures to be attracted here was Dr Johnson in 1745. Nearby on the right is number 13 which has a blue plaque to Henry Hyndman, founder of the Social Democratic Federation, who lived and died here. Opposite is number 40, also marked by a plaque, which was artist John Constable's last home. On the corner is the Wells Tavern which began as a hotel for spa visitors.

Turn left at the Wells to walk down Christchurch Hill to find Preachers Hill, part of the Heath, on the left. At the bottom, by a horse trough, continue ahead along Willow Road. Number 2, the last building on the right, was designed as his own home by emigré Hungarian architect Ernö Goldfinger in 1937. It nearly failed to get planning permission but now it is in the care of the National Trust. Turn right for another out of place building – the Freemasons Arms.

7 Highgate
The Flask

There were plenty of pubs in Highgate because the viewpoint village was an overnight stop for men driving cattle to Smithfield's live meat market. The milestone at the top of West Hill gives the distance from 'St Giles Pound'. Nearby is the Flask which dates from at least 1716 and takes its name from the flasks which could be obtained here for filling with spring water on the far side of Hampstead Heath. The swearing on the horns ceremony, involving a drover's oath, is carried out here annually. Highwayman Dick Turpin is said to have hidden in the cellars and artist William Hogarth did an instant sketch of a distorted face after a fellow drinker had been hit in the face with a tankard during a quarrel. Also claimed as a former customer is Karl Marx, who is buried in the cemetery at the bottom of Swains Lane.

This is a celebrated Taylor Walker pub which has been an *Evening Standard* Pub of the Year. Inside are small, low ceilinged rooms with pictures of old Highgate on the walls. There are two bars, one with a sash hatch, and windowless cellars at the back. But many go no further than the front courtyard where there are tables

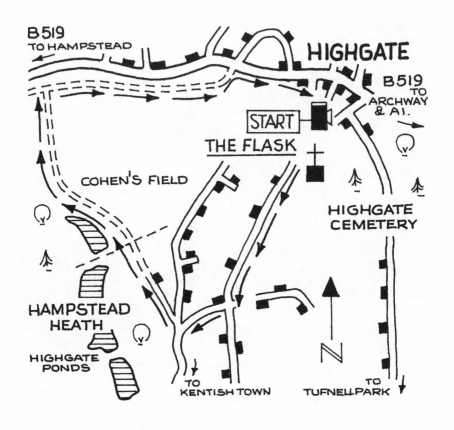

in summer and a brazier in winter. There is a long menu with Cheddar, ham, beef or Stilton ploughman's, filled petit pain, jacket potatoes, salads, Greek platter and steak and ale pie. There is usually a vegetarian dish too. Drinks include coffee, pots of tea and Flask Bouka (hot chocolate with rum and whipped cream). This is a Taylor Walker house serving Ind Coope's Burton Ale, Tetley Bitter, Young's Bitter, Young's Special and Winter Warmer.

The Flask is open all day from 11 am to 11 pm with food served from 12 noon to 9.15 pm. The Sunday opening times are 12 noon to 10.30 pm.

Telephone: 0181 340 7260.

How to get there: Highgate is on the B519 north up the hill from

Archway. The nearest Underground station is Highgate. Bus 240 runs up the hill to the village from Archway station. Bus 246 from King's Cross passes the pub at the top of Highgate West Hill, N6.

Parking: There is no car park at the pub but very limited on street parking is available.

Length of the walk: 2 miles. Map: A-Z London Street Map; OS Pathfinder 1159 City of London; OS Landranger 176 West London (inn GR 283872).

Highgate still gives the impression of being outside London and the view from the hilltop village encourages this feeling. Dick Whittington was about to climb the hill when he heard the bells of the City calling him and his cat back. Later Nell Gwynne escaped the capital to come here with her baby and live in Lauderdale House. As a child John Betjeman lived on West Hill and saw sheep being driven up the hill. This walk goes down the hill to find a former farm track where great literary figures once strolled, to Kenwood which poet Coleridge described as 'beyond compare the loveliest place near London'.

The Walk

From the Flask turn left to cross a road and bear right past St Michael's church, London's highest church, where poet Samuel Taylor Coleridge is buried in the central aisle. A mark in the porch indicates that this spot is level with the top of St Paul's Cathedral. Walk on past the milestone to go downhill. Across the road is the entrance to the huge Witanhurst mansion rebuilt in 1913 for Liberal MP Sir Arthur Crosfield. Just after passing the YHA (left) look across the road to see a brick plaque on number 40 recalling the Fox and Crown inn where the young Queen Victoria rested after the landlord had stopped her carriage's bolting horses. Victoria, who was in the second week of her long reign, granted the Fox the right to display her arms.

After the bend go right down Merton Lane to reach the edge of Hampstead Heath. Below can be seen the wide expanse of Highgate's boating pond. Go right, but not sharp right, along Millfield Lane – a signpost points to Fitzroy Farm. This lane was called 'Poets Lane' by essayist Leigh Hunt and certainly it was known to his friend, the poet John Keats, who on different occasions met Coleridge and essayist William Hazlitt here.

Soon through the trees on the left can be seen Kenwood Ladies' Bathing Pond where actress Margaret Rutherford used to swim every morning. At a 'crossroads' keep forward with another of the Highgate ponds to the left. On emerging from the trees, there is the expanse of grass known as Cohen's Fields to the right. Stay on the main path which curves uphill. To the left is the ground used for Kenwood's famous open-air concerts.

The path becomes rougher and shortly there is a brief view of Kenwood House. In the 18th century this was the country seat of Lord Mansfield, Lord Chief Justice, whose London home was in Bloomsbury Square. He called in the Adam brothers to restyle Kenwood which remained in the family until 1924. Under English Heritage it is open most days for visitors to view the Iveagh Bequest, the most important private collection of paintings. Rembrandt, Reynolds, Gainsborough and Turner are all represented.

At the T-junction the house is to the left. The walk continues to the right towards a golden topped shelter but before reaching it there is a view of Highgate on the hill and then a panoramic view of London unfolds.

At the next path junction go ahead down the rough narrow track which runs along the side of the meadow. At the far end go left to find the path suddenly metalled. The way is now through an area known as the Orchard. At the road, Hampstead Lane, go right to pass between Highgate school playing fields on the left and the high wall of Athlone House on the right. It is a gentle climb up into Highgate. Go right at the first turning, The Grove. As indicated by the two plaques, at different times Coleridge and novelist J.B. Priestley lived at number 3. More recently, violinist Yehudi Menuhin lived next door at number 2. Opposite is the Flask.

Primrose Hill
The Swans at Coole

There was some criticism when this pub changed its name from the Princess of Wales to the Swans at Coole in 1994. But there is a local reason for naming the pub after W.B. Yeats' poem *The Wild Swans at Coole*. The poet and dramatist lived a few yards away at 23 Fitzroy Road from 1867 to 1873 during early childhood.

The Swans at Coole is now cool with a pale green decor, large plain windows and even a fan for hot days. The seating is largely redundant church pews grouped around tables. Even as the Princess, the food and atmosphere had the feel of a bistro. Now the soup is called potage. The deep fried potatoes in skins come with a shredded chicken or chilli salsa and a topping of melted cheese along with a sour cream and chive dip. Also on the menu are pizza, pasta, salad and steak. At the circular central bar there are 18 wines available as well as Boddingtons and Flowers ales including Colonel Pepper's Lemon Ale. Cappuccino is among the six coffees and seven teas served.

The Swans at Coole is open all day from 11 am to 11 pm. Sunday hours are 12 noon to 10.30 pm.

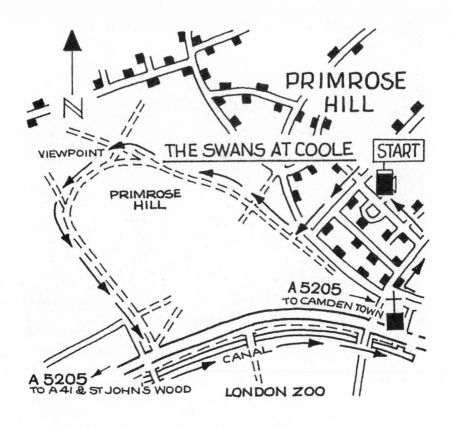

Telephone: 0171 722 0354.

How to get there: Primrose Hill is to the west of Camden Town and by car is best reached by way of the A5205 Prince Albert Road and Albert Terrace at the side of Primrose Hill. There is no vehicle access from Chalk Farm but Chalk Farm Underground station is the nearest station. The pub is on the corner of Chalcot Road and Fitzroy Road which runs between Regent's Park Road and Gloucester Road.

Parking: There is no car park at the pub but very limited on street parking is available.

Length of the walk: 2 miles. Map: A-Z London Street Map; OS

Pathfinder 1159 City of London; OS Landranger 176 West London (inn GR 282840).

Primrose Hill is both the 206 ft viewpoint and the very attractive London village squashed below the hill's east side. There are numerous unusual shops and cafés which is why the Swans at Coole is not out of place. The walk goes first to the top of the hill for the view across London to the hill beyond Dulwich. The route back is by way of the Regent's Canal and the zoo.

The Walk

From the corner pub cross Chalcot Road to pass the corner café and walk down Fitzroy Road towards the Primrose Hill grass. After a short distance there is W.B. Yeats' house on the left, easily identified by the blue plaque. At the far end cross Regent's Park Road using the crossing and enter the park, which was forest until cleared for meadowland during Elizabeth I's reign. The name probably comes from the flowers which grew in the old woodland here. In the early 19th century this was a popular duelling ground.

Turn right to walk up the hill. Keep forward at a junction to pass two parish stones on the left (marking the St Pancras–St Marylebone border) and take the next turning on the left to walk up to the viewpoint. Looking south from here can be seen St Paul's Cathedral, St Pancras station, Parliament's Big Ben and Victoria Tower, Westminster Cathedral and the Crystal Palace radio mast. Immediately below is London Zoo's huge aviary.

To walk down the hill turn round and continue on the path, keeping left at the two junctions before going left on to the long straight path running downhill. At the bottom of the hill there is Primrose Hill Lodge at Prince Albert Road.

Cross the road and turn right for a short distance before going left into Regent's Park. Just before the bridge bear right to follow a path down to the Regent's Canal towpath. Walk under the bridge to follow the canal through the zoo. There may be some animals to be seen across the water. The canal opened in 1820 linking Little Venice with the Thames. Steam tugs operated here and in 1874 one carrying gunpowder blew up by the zoo, which had opened just eight years after the canal was dug. Soon beside the towpath is the aviary designed by Lord Snowdon and opened in 1964.

Soon after the riverbus stop on the far bank, you find on the

View of London and the zoo from Primrose Hill.

towpath side the boundary markers for St Marylebone and St Pancras parishes. Ahead is Cumberland Basin where the main canal traffic turns north to pass under the road. This sharp bend is a result of last minute doubts about the canal being dug through the middle of Regent's Park. The basin is the remains of an arm which ran down the east side of Regent's Park to Cumberland hay market until filled with bomb rubble during the Second World War. The large oriental style craft is a floating Chinese restaurant.

Walk up to Water Meeting Bridge to go left and right into St Mark's Square. On the corner is St Mark's church, consecrated in 1853 and noted for having a reredos by Ninian Comper behind both the high and Lady chapel altars and some Comper windows. A more modern window, depicting a Sputnik, is claimed as the first to feature a space rocket.

At the crossroads with Regent's Park Road continue ahead down Princess Road. Turn left into Chalcot Road to find the the Swans at Coole at the next crossroads.

9 High Holborn
The Cittie of Yorke

Refreshment has been offered on this site since 1430. By 1695 it was known as the Gray's Inn Coffee House and the cellar bar is said to have been part of the original coffee house. The last major rebuilding was in 1923. Until recently its name was Henekey's Long Bar – the main bar is said to be one of the longest in Britain – but the present name comes from a pub which was once part of Staple Inn across the road.

The Cittie of Yorke backs on to Gray's Inn so there are often plenty of members of the legal profession. Indeed, the main hall's small cubicles were originally intended for lawyers wanting to discuss court business with clients. The huge wine butts are also redundant but until the Second World War each held 1,000 gallons. The three-sided stove with an under floor flue dates from the time of the Battle of Waterloo and was originally in the hall of Gray's Inn. A smaller bar at the front is decorated with pictures of York through the ages.

At lunchtime food is available upstairs and down with a regular menu of ploughman's, filled baps and salads. Specials sometimes include Cumberland sausage in sauce, with chips. Appropriately, the Cittie of Yorke is in the hands of Samuel Smith, Yorkshire's oldest brewery, so Samuel Smith's Old Brewery Bitter and Museum Ale are served.

The Cittie of Yorke is open 11.30 am to 11 pm weekdays except for Saturday when there is an afternoon closure 3.30 pm to 5.30 pm. No Sunday opening. Food is available downstairs in the evening from 5.30 pm except on Saturdays.

Telephone: 0171 242 7670.

How to get there: High Holborn runs between Holborn Kingsway and Chancery Lane Underground stations. The Cittie of Yorke is at number 22 on the north side near the junction with Chancery Lane and a few yards west of Chancery Lane station.

Parking: There is no parking at the pub or in the immediate vicinity.

Length of the walk: 1 mile. Map: A-Z London Street Map; OS Pathfinder 1159 City of London; OS Landranger 176 West London and 177 East London (inn GR 309817).

This central London walk explores the alleyways which lie behind the vast Prudential building, Holborn. Here is London's Italian quarter, known as Little Italy, and jewellery centre, better known as Hatton Garden. There are also two historic churches and a private gated street.

The Walk
Turn left out of the pub to pass an entrance to Gray's Inn, a legal centre since the 14th century. Its gardens are the last of the great gardens found here in Tudor times. Cross Gray's Inn Road (there is a subway). Opposite this T-junction is Staple Inn which was built in 1586 for the wool trade.

Go left into Brooke Street and after a few yards look up on the left wall for a plaque marking the spot where 17 year old poet Thomas Chatterton was found dead in 1770. At the far end of the street is Brooke's Market and the archway entrance to St Alban's church which frames a sculpture of the Risen Christ by Hans Feibusch, whose dramatic mural can be seen inside the church.

Bear right and go left under another archway and walk down narrow Leigh Place. The new building is the award winning St Alban's Centre by architect Gordon Fleming. Ahead is Baldwin's Gardens, a street named after Elizabeth I's gardener Richard Baldwin who had his own garden here. Turn right along Baldwin's Gardens to reach Leather Lane and go left. This ancient street, which was the western boundary of the Ely House garden, has a market every weekday lunchtime. The Continental Stores on the right near the end is a reminder that this is the edge of Little Italy where Italians have gathered since the 1860s.

At the Clock House go right into Hatton Wall which marks the northern boundary of the garden attached to Ely House.

A passage off Ely Place, with iron pole to discourage horse riding

Shakespeare's *Richard III* mentions the strawberries which grew here at the time when it belonged to the Bishop of Ely. In the 1580s much of it was rented by Elizabeth I's favourite Sir Christopher Hatton who built himself a house. The short street soon reaches the famous Hatton Garden – the road which runs down the middle of the former garden.

At the crossroads with Hatton Garden look left to see Terroni & Sons which is next to St Peter's Italian church, built in 1863 to resemble St Crisogono in Rome's Trastevere district. Turn right to walk down Hatton Garden which has been a well known diamond and jewellery centre since gold and silver engravers started work here in the 1830s. The chapel on the corner of Cross Street was built as a temporary replacement for St Andrew's Holborn which was destroyed in the 1666 Great Fire of London. Just before reaching Holborn Circus look for a blue doorway on the left between numbers 9 and 10 leading to Ye Olde Mitre pub.

Go through the doorway and along the passage to pass the Mitre which was built in 1546 to serve the Bishop of Ely's staff. Through the corner window it is just possible to see the remains of a cherry tree around which Elizabeth I danced one May Day. The central pole at the far end of the alley is to discourage horses from turning up here from Ely Place. Go left to find St Etheldreda's, England's oldest Roman Catholic church dating from 1251, and the only remaining part of Ely House – the London residence of the Bishop of Ely for 500 years.

To leave Ely Place, a private street, walk to the south end where there is a lodge and a view of St Andrew's Holborn, rebuilt to Wren's design after the Great Fire – the wind changed to save St Etheldreda's. Outside the gates go right up to Holborn Circus where there is 'London's politest statue'– Prince Albert raising his hat. Continue across the entrance to Hatton Garden and up Holborn to pass the end of Leather Lane and the red terracotta Prudential headquarters designed by Alfred Waterhouse and dating from 1876. The public may enter the gates during weekday daylight hours to view Waterhouse Square where there is a bust of Charles Dickens who lived on the site.

Continue along Holborn and across the end of Gray's Inn Road (or through the subway), to reach the Cittie of Yorke.

10 Cockfosters
The Cock and Dragon

This used to be just the Cock but since being taken over by Dragon Inns the name has been the Cock and Dragon. Cockfosters, which in the 19th century was 'Cock Fosters' probably means 'home of the chief forester'. The pub's Thirties style exterior, with its weathercock on top of the clock tower, looks rather out of place at the eastern gateway to Hadley Common.

It was different in 1930 when John Betjeman spent a summer evening sitting on a wooden bench outside enjoying three halves. He recalled his visit in his poem *Cricket Master* and described the journey from nearby Cat Hill: 'Sweet bean-fields then were scenting Middlesex;/Narrow lanes led between the diary-farms/To ponds reflecting weather-boarded inns'.

The inside is a surprise with its panelled walls, cosy corners including the fireplace, stained glass and homely china displays. In the evenings the lighting is low and, although there is now one rather than two bars, the Cock remains a quiet pub. At the back there is a garden which makes up for the severe forecourt.

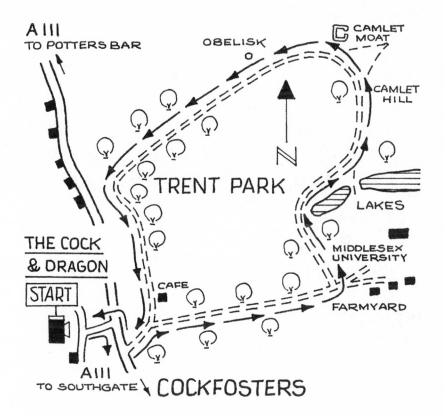

The only significant change made by Dragon Inns is the menu which is mainly Thai. At lunchtime there is an Oriental Express menu which offers a huge choice including sesame minced chicken on toast, roasted pork spare ribs with honey, spicy fishcakes and steamed dim sum dumplings. There are plenty of vegetarian dishes. Snacks include Monks Vegetarian Platter. There is also a separate Thai restaurant.

As this was a Benskins house, there is still Benskins Best Bitter as well as imported Thai beers. Also available are Ind Coope's Burton Ale, Tetley Bitter and Wadworth 6X.

The opening times are 11 am to 11 pm. Food is served 12 noon to 2.30 pm and 7 pm to 10.30 pm except Sunday evening. Sunday opening hours are 12 noon to 3 pm and 7 pm to 10.30 pm.

Telephone: 0181 449 7160.

How to get there: The Cock and Dragon is in Chalk Lane off the A111 at Cockfosters, which is between Southgate and Potters Bar. Cockfosters Underground station is nearby.

Parking: There is a large forecourt car park.

Length of the walk: 2¾ miles. Map: A-Z London Street Map; OS Pathfinder 1140 Barnet & Enfield; OS Landranger 176 West London (inn GR 278966).

Cockfosters is the last station on the Piccadilly Line which runs alongside the huge Trent Park estate. This country park, with ancient woodland and fields harvested for hay to encourage grassland flowers, provides a perfect oasis for a walk from the pub, which is placed between the Park and Hadley Common – both once part of the Enfield Chase hunting ground. Even a walk up the long drive to the farmyard behind the lodge and back is rewarding. The full route takes in the woods and farmland.

The Walk
From the pub forecourt go ahead down Chalk Lane to the main road. Turn right and after a short distance go left through the gates of Trent Park. The name comes from Trento in the Austrian Tyrol where George III's doctor, Sir Richard Jebb, saved the life of the Duke of Gloucester. The grateful king allowed the doctor to purchase part of the Enfield Chase hunting ground which was being broken up due to massive poaching by gangs coming out from London. It was still considered rural enough in 1935 for the present Duke of Kent's father to spend part of his honeymoon here. Then the house belonged to Sir Philip Sassoon who employed 18 gardeners. After his death at the outbreak of the Second World War the mansion became an interrogation centre for captured enemy airmen including Rudolph Hess.

Now the building is part of Middlesex University and the 360 acre grounds, laid out by Humphrey Repton with grass and woodland, are open to the public. Follow the main drive by keeping to the footpath on the right. At the junction by an obelisk keep right. The drive now runs straight ahead. As an alternative to the tarmac there is a parallel path running through the trees on each side. The trees were planted by the Bevan family who came into the estate in 1833 when banker David Bevan nodded whilst asleep at an auction.

After ½ mile there is ancient woodland and a lodge now used as an information point. Behind the lodge is the farmyard inhabited by goats, sheep, pigs, rabbits, chickens and ducks.

The walk continues to the left where the rough path is signposted 'Lakes and Water Garden'. The path runs gently downhill just inside the wood. At a junction in the open keep forward and follow the path round to the right to find the lake. The path continues above the waterside sweep of grass. Just before the next junction there is a view left of an obelisk in the trees (reached later) and right up to the mansion. Keep forward ignoring the two right turnings. The way is uphill with a fine view behind, to become metalled and enter a wood. Before the way bears round to the right take the small turning half left. After being joined by another path there is a fence in the trees to the right marking the (hard to discern) Camlet Moat which features in Sir Walter Scott's *The Fortunes of Nigel* as the scene of Lord Dalgano's murder.

At the next junction, where farmland can be seen through the thin trees, go left and shortly on the right there is the huge obelisk commemorating the birth in 1732 of a son to an earlier Duke and Duchess of Kent – note the spelling of 'duchess'. The infant Earl of Harold lived for just a few months. From here there is the best view of the mansion. The obelisk, first erected in Wrest Park in Bedfordshire, was brought here in 1933 to improve the view from the house.

Continue through the woods and at a junction take the right fork to keep ahead. The path now runs down and uphill alongside a field. There is a view of a water tower (reached later). At the far end the path veers left to run through trees on the edge of the estate. Beyond the water tower go left and right to pass a covered reservoir. Keep forward past the café (behind a hedge on the left) to join the driveway by the small obelisk.

Follow the drive back to the main road and go right and then left to reach the Cock and Dragon.

11 Southgate
The Woodman

The Woodman was built on top of a hill as two cottages and still looks like a small residence. A retired policeman living here in 1868 managed to obtain a licence and it has been a pub ever since. Inside the front door are the small bar and homely bookshelves. The low beamed room opposite, once a separate home, is the sitting area. This is little changed and old photographs on the wall show the cottage covered in ivy.

The menu is chalked up on a board propped up on the bar counter and, as befits a cottage, the food is home-made. Naturally there is sometimes cottage pie as well as lasagne, sandwiches including popular Stilton and hot bacon, toasted sandwiches featuring ham, cheese and tomato and jacket potatoes with various toppings.

This remains a freehouse which maintains its old link with Whitbread by having beers from the Whitbread guest list – Whitbread Boddingtons Bitter, Greene King Abbot, Morland Old Speckled Hen and Flowers IPA. The opening hours are 12 noon to 3 pm and 5.30 pm to 11 pm. On Saturdays it is open all day from 11 am. The Sunday hours are 12 noon to 3 pm and 7 pm to 10.30 pm. Telephone: 0181 886 6250.

How to get there: The Woodman is on Bourne Hill, N21 on the A111 between Southgate and Edmonton. Bus W9, linking Southgate and Winchmore Hill stations, passes the door. The nearest Underground station is Southgate.

Parking: There is a car park at the side of the pub and parking is allowed in the street.

Length of the walk: 2 miles. Map: A-Z London Street Map; OS Pathfinder 1140 Barnet & Enfield; OS Landranger 176 West London or 177 East London (inn GR 304938).

Bourne Hill retains not only its attractive old pub but its cattle pound. Behind the Woodman is a remnant of the ancient Forest of Middlesex which survived as part of an estate belonging to a brandy merchant whose name lives on as a famous brewery. The walk explores this surviving parkland countryside and passes some attractive historic cottages near the church.

The Walk
Turn right out of the pub and walk down Bourne Hill to the grand entrance to Grovelands Park. Follow the main park path ahead and where the way divides bear right down to the lake inhabited by ducks and water-hens. Soon there is a view over to the left of a large classical mansion on high ground. This is Grovelands, designed by John Nash and built in 1797-8 for brandy merchant Walker Gray. The estate later passed to his relative John Taylor. The two names live on with the Taylor Walker brewery. The house, a hospital since 1921, has won a Civic Trust Award for its renovation. The parkland, landscaped by Humphrey Repton, has been open to the public since 1913.

Continue alongside the lake and at the junction of paths at the end keep forward. In the trees to the right is the stream fed by the lake. At a junction by tennis courts still keep ahead to pass the bowling green house and reach the gates by a road. Turn right to walk up Church Hill. On the way there are the Woodside Cottages – white weatherboarded houses including the Old School House dating from 1785 and used as a school until 1859.

Further uphill is the impressive St Paul's church opened in 1828, on land donated by Walker Gray, when this area was part of the parish of Edmonton. The church is noted for its early Victorian stained glass. The chancel was added in 1888.

Turn right into Denleigh Gardens and at the crossroads go right again down Branscombe Gardens to re-enter Grovelands Park. At once leave the metalled path by going left on a well used footpath through the beech and oak trees. Cross a second metalled path and when the fence on the left turns away bear half right across to the stream. Follow the stream (right) and continue by the long waterfall to climb steeply up to the lake. Turn left to walk round the

Woodside Cottages

east side of the lake. At the corner there is a view of the mansion.

At the far end of the lake, as the path begins to turn, go sharp left on a path which climbs up through the oaks near the golf course (right). At the top of the slope go right on to a metalled path running between wire and wooden fences. The way briefly opens out before emerging between two houses at Bourne Hill Road. Opposite is the cattle pound last used in 1904 when the pinders (pound caretakers) were the Woodman's landlord and his wife. Go right to reach the Woodman.

12 Alexandra Palace
The Phoenix

The Alexandra Palace, completed in 1873 and named after Princess Alexandra of Denmark who had married the future Edward VII, was intended as a recreation centre. It is still a venue for concerts, meetings and exhibitions. A blue plaque beneath the radio tower at the east end recalls the transmission of the first television programmes in 1935 from this high point.

At the opposite end is the unexpected pub, which opened in 1989 in a corner of Alexandra Palace following renovation after the 1980 fire. This had mirrored a devastating fire just over a century earlier which is recorded in prints around the bar. So there is a double reason for the name and bird on the pub sign outside.

Children are welcome in the indoor patio at the back which is really part of the magnificent glass roofed Palm Court complete with palms and terracotta reliefs. From the terrace at the front there is a panoramic view across London to Crystal Palace in the south. In summer the dome of St Paul's Cathedral appears as if surrounded by trees. Nearer to the east is Highgate with its dome of St Joseph's on the southern slope – also seen on the Hampstead pub walk.

The main high ceilinged central bar has been described as 'Gatsby style' and has live jazz on Sundays.

The lunchtime menu offers only one ploughman's – the traditional cheese, but there are jacket potatoes with salad toppings, chicken dishes and jumbo sausage with French bread. This freehouse has Fuller's London Pride, Ind Coope's Burton Ale and Tetley Bitter.

The Phoenix is open all day 11 am to 11 pm and Sundays 12 noon to 10.30 pm.

Telephone: 0181 365 2121.

How to get there: Alexandra Palace is in Alexandra Park which has a road running past the Palace linking the A504 at Muswell Hill with Wood Green. Bus W3 runs between Wood Green Underground station and Alexandra Palace.

Parking: There is no parking available at the pub but there is a public car park nearby in the park.

Length of the walk: 2½ miles. Map: A-Z London Street Map; OS Pathfinder 1159 City of London; OS Landranger 176 West London (inn GR 896298).

The route is through the woods seen from the pub's viewpoint. A former railway line, now the Parkland Walk and a nature conservation corridor, provides a rural way down to Highgate Woods. The return is by way of Queen's Wood and a good footpath giving a fine view back to the viewpoint which is reached with only brief contact with buildings.

The Walk

Leave the Phoenix by the side door under the pub sign and go down the steps to the road. Go ahead on the road but as it bends to the left downhill keep forward. There is a signpost pointing to a cafeteria and bandstand. The way ahead has two gates to stop traffic. At a junction go left up an avenue of trees. At a second path junction go left to go under a covered way which bends to take the path to the side of Muswell Hill.

Turn left at a T-junction to walk under Muswell Hill and join the line of the railway which carried passengers from Highgate to

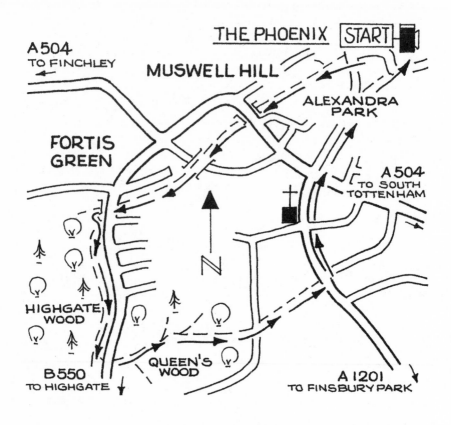

Alexandra Palace from 1873 until 1954. Much of the building material for Muswell Hill housing arrived by rail. Soon there is a view over Hornsey and Crouch End from a viaduct. The Canary Wharf tower is half left and to the north is the spire of St James's Muswell Hill. The path runs through a wooded cutting to pass under Muswell Hill Road. Ahead was Cranley Gardens station. Bear left to join the road and before the shops go right through Highgate Wood's Cranley Gate.

At the junction go left . At the second junction there is a lodge with a Corporation of London shield over the door reminding us that the woods were saved by the City in 1885. At the third four-way junction bear left and then left again down to New Gate by Muswell Hill Road.

Cross over to enter Queen's Wood which was opened to the public in 1898 to mark Queen Victoria's Diamond Jubilee the previous year. It had been known as Churchyard Bottom which may be a reference to pits dug centuries before for the burial of plague victims. The woodland path runs downhill to a junction. Take the right fork to continue downhill to the valley floor. Having crossed the stream (sometimes dry in summer) at once turn left on to a narrow path which follows the ditch. Keep forward at a pond and continue on the woodland path. On reaching a low wall go round the end to follow a metalled path which crosses a road. The path runs straight ahead and is lined for much of the ¼ mile with blackberry bushes. Each side are tennis courts and over to the left first a view of Alexandra Palace on the hill and then St James's Muswell Hill.

At Park Road turn left. Soon on the left there is the modern Hornsey parish church. Beyond here at the crossroads is the Victoria Stakes pub recalling the racecourse which was once at the bottom of Alexandra Park. Using the crossings make for the arched entrance to Alexandra Park opposite.

Stay on the right to go under the arch and turn on to a parallel footpath behind a line of trees. Follow the path which later winds a little to meet a side road. Turn left past a barrier and before the main park road turn right up a footpath. At the top of the slope go left to the road. Opposite are Alexandra Palace and the Phoenix.

13 Enfield Town
The Crown and Horseshoes

Enfield's Crown and Horseshoes is on a bend of the New River and only seen at the last minute by walkers on the riverside path. Although hard to find it is known by many who appreciate its unusual setting. Here the water is now only a loop on the New River so the flow is reduced but this channel proved vital for London's water supply in the Second World War when the direct pipe section to the east of Enfield was bombed.

The pub dates from at least the early 19th century. In December 1832 essayist Charles Lamb was a witness in a murder investigation which involved a group of men he had seen drinking here with a merchant seaman later found dead nearby.

This is a cottage style pub, reached by a bridge, with one bar and a conservatory for eating. The large garden, which in summer becomes the main eating and drinking area, has twice won the Crown and Horseshoes the annual 'Outside Inn' award. There are full disabled facilities for those visiting the pub and its garden.

Sandwiches include chicken tikka and the puddings list often features spotted dick. On Sundays there is a roast lunch on the

menu. This is a Whitbread house serving Whitbread Boddingtons Bitter, Flowers Original, Brakspear Bitter and guest beers.
The opening hours are 11 am to 11 pm with food available 12 noon to 3 pm and 5.30 pm to 9.30 pm. The Sunday hours are 12 noon to 10.30 pm with food available until about 5 pm.
Telephone: 0181 363 1371.

How to get there: The Crown and Horseshoes is at the end of Horseshoes Lane off Chase Side which runs north in Enfield from the A110 between Cockfosters and the A10 Great Cambridge Road. Enfield Chase and Enfield Town BR stations are nearby.

Parking: There is no parking at or near the inn which must be approached on foot but limited parking is available at Chase Side.

Length of the walk: 1½ miles. Map: A-Z Master Atlas of Greater London; OS Pathfinder 1140 Barnet & Enfield; OS Landranger West London 176 or East London 177 (inn GR 325969).

Enfield existed before the Norman conquest. The manor house was large enough to be called a 'Palace'. Into the 20th century there were extensive orchards and nurseries here to feed the capital. This was the home town of Disraeli's father who was born on the site of what is now Enfield Town station booking hall where a plaque recalls that Keats went to school in the same building. This is a short walk round a little town which retains its character. The cottages are as delightful as any found in Hampstead but here they have the added attraction of being on the banks of the 400 year old man-made New River dug to bring fresh water to London.

The Walk
On leaving the pub cross the footbridge and go left along the riverside path. After passing a gated bridge take the next one to cross the water again and go down a passage into Gentleman's Row. Keep on the left side of the attractive street and after the way narrows look for the black and white house, the 17th-century Clarendon Cottage, marked with a discreet plaque. This is where essayist and humorist Charles Lamb and his mentally ill sister lived from 1825 to 1827 before moving to nearby Chase Side.
The path leads to a junction by the Stag pub. Turn right to pass

63

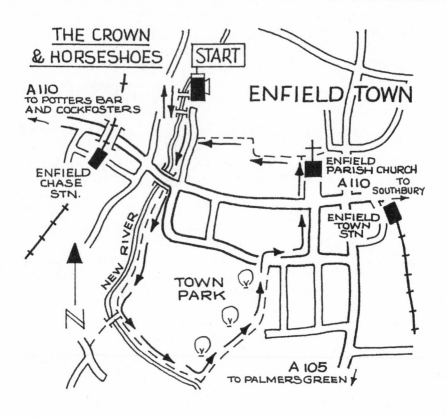

the pub frontage and Trinity church. Cross the crossing in front of the church. Once on the far side go right for a few yards to a bridge. Do not cross the New River but go left on a path running between the river and River House.

Stay on this path and soon there is a park on the left. Where the river turns sharp left do not go over the bridge but turn left to go through a gate and follow the water along the top end of the park. On the far side of the water is a natural bank with a golf course beyond. This is a good spot to see water-hens, Canada geese and even large fish such as carp or tench. There is a view back to town from this man-made river on high ground.

Where the path ends bear left down the side of the park – a path runs behind the trees. At the imposing gated park entrance keep forward on a path which is metalled all the way to the small gate on to Cecil Road.

Turn right and at the crossing cross over to go left (ahead from the crossing) down the side of Marks & Spencer. At the far end use another crossing to cross Church Street. Directly ahead is the Market Place and Enfield parish church.

The church, dedicated to St Andrew, dates from the 13th century. In Tudor times there was a meat market outside on Sunday mornings but now market day is Saturday.

Go down the passage which runs between the King's Head and the church. At a junction go left into Holly Walk and stay on this path as it double bends (ignore a turning) to meet Gentleman's Row. Go right to find the New River. Cross the bridge and turn right to find the Crown and Horseshoes.

14 Tottenham
The Antwerp Arms

The Antwerp Arms was built about 1820 facing fields and trees and the view from the front door is still the grass of the Bruce Castle grounds. This is a little known, rural corner of Tottenham and the walls of the pub have pictures of past times, including local scenes. The pub, built in advance of the 1843 cottages next door, was just a beerhouse until the late 1870s when Charringtons called it the Antwerp Arms – possibly following success at a beer festival.

Inside there are traditional round, iron frame, pub tables, although the ones outside in the garden are wooden. There is a conservatory at the back looking over little back gardens.

The home-cooked food changes daily and customers must look at a menu chalked in different colours above one end of the single bar. There are always plenty of sandwiches and sometimes a hot meat variety as well as jacket potatoes with various fillings. The main dishes can be scampi, steak, omelettes and ham, egg and chips. Occasionally there is a meringue and whipped cream pudding. Traditional roast lunch is popular on Sundays. The Antwerp Arms, once *Evening Standard* Pub of the Year, is a Charringtons house with Draught Bass and Worthington Best Bitter always available.

The Antwerp Arms is open 11 am to 11 pm with meals available until 2.30 pm. The Sunday opening hours are 12 noon to 10.30 pm. Telephone: 0181 808 4449.

How to get there: The Antwerp Arms is in Church Road, N17 behind Bruce Castle, which is on the A109 Lordship Lane between Wood Green and Tottenham's High Road. Church Lane at the side of Bruce Castle leads to Church Road. Bruce Grove and White Hart Lane BR stations are nearby.

Parking: There is no car park at the pub but there is on street parking available.

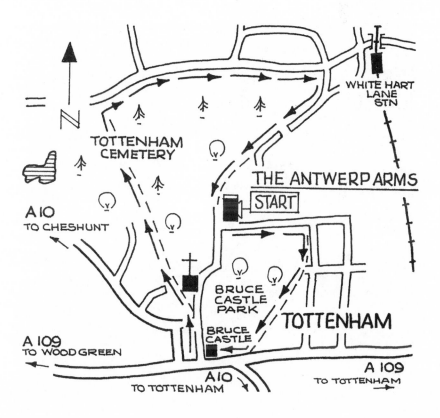

Bruce Castle – dating from the reign of Charles II but now a local history museum.

Length of the walk: 1½ miles. Map: A-Z London Street Map; OS Pathfinder 1140 Barnet & Enfield; OS Landranger 177 East London (inn GR 336911).

Bruce Castle is a magnificent sight for anyone approaching the north end of Bruce Grove. Here in the middle of north London the Stuart house still retains its country setting, which is explored on this walk. This is a short route but the tour can easily fill an afternoon when Bruce Castle and the church are open. The park and footpath to White Hart Lane are rich in wildlife.

The Walk

There is a gate into the park directly opposite the pub but, to avoid climbing the low wall and walking on the sometimes soft ground, go left to the end of the park and turn right down New Road. Beyond the playground there is a gateway. Follow the middle path across the park to reach Bruce Castle.

The present house dates from Charles II's reign when Lord Coleraine rebuilt an existing manor house but its name recalls Robert the Bruce who owned the manor for a brief period at the end of the 13th century. Henry VIII met his sister Margaret, Queen of Scots here in 1516 and his daughter Elizabeth I visited in 1568. In Tudor times, Bruce Castle was a country refuge from the plague outbreaks in London. The Castle is now the Borough of Haringey's local history museum (open Wednesday to Sunday afternoons). The impressive display of post boxes is in honour of Penny Post and adhesive stamp founder Rowland Hill who ran a school at the house from 1827 to 1833. On the stairs is a painting by John Bonny of 'The cottage near Church Path, White Hart Lane' – a spot passed later on this walk.

Walk along the front of Bruce Castle by the front door to pass the 14th- century tower. Its origin is a mystery although it may have been a dovecote. One of Lord Coleraine's wives is said to have been locked inside and jumped from the battlements – her ghostly form is said to be seen repeating the feat on the anniversary each November.

At Church Lane go right. Just before the church there is The Priory on the left. This Georgian fronted house, built in 1620 for a barber surgeon in the City of London, is now the vicarage of All Hallows next door. Turn into the churchyard to find a scene attractive enough to have moved John Constable to paint the ancient church whilst staying in Tottenham in 1806. The tower is 14th-century and the 15th-century porch is built with local bricks. (Flower pots were still made nearby until 1961.)

Continue through the churchyard and past the west end tower to find a straight path running north through Tottenham cemetery. The fenced path is lined with trees as it runs for ¼ mile through the rural oasis. At the far end the path crosses the Moselle stream (which flows from Muswell Hill) before widening to meet White Hart Lane. Look at the 'Good Rule and Government Byelaw' notice on the left warning against riding tricycles on the White Hart Lane pavements.

White Hart Lane, which has given its name to the nearby Tottenham Hotspur Football Club ground, links Wood Green and Tottenham. Turn right to walk past the T-junction into Creighton Road – this was built as a short cut on the winding White Hart Lane. When the road becomes White Hart Lane again turn right (before the Railway Tavern) up Beaufoy Road.

Keep on the right-hand side and soon the pavement is alongside the cemetery. At the sharp left bend keep ahead down the narrow path which leads to Prospect Place. Look up to see the date 1822 on the cottages. At the road go left to reach the Antwerp Arms.

⑮ Canonbury
The Compton Arms

This tiny pub in the mews behind Canonbury Terrace has hardly changed over the last few decades and it is still quiet enough to sit outside the front door in the summer. At the back there is a courtyard with a sycamore tree. Inside, the television may be showing a test match or football. The walls are decorated with local prints and photographs.

The food choice is chalked up on a board by the bar and includes Cheddar, Brie and ham ploughman's, pâté and hot toast with salad, pasties and fish. Jacket potatoes come with tuna, cheese or sweetcorn and coleslaw toppings. Until the early Eighties this was still a freehouse but now as a Greene King house there are Greene King XX Mild, Greene King IPA, Rayments Special, Abbot and, in season, Winter Ale.

The opening times are 11 am to 11 pm with food available all the time. The Sunday hours are 12 noon to 3 pm and 7 pm to 10.30 pm but food is not served.

Telephone: 0171 359 2645.

How to get there: The Compton Arms is in Compton Avenue,

N1 which runs between Highbury Corner roundabout and Canonbury Square. Highbury Corner is on the A1 north of The Angel. At Highbury Corner is Highbury & Islington BR & Underground station.

Parking: There is no car park at the pub but there is limited on street parking available nearby.

Length of the walk: 2½ miles. Map: A-Z London Street Map; OS Pathfinder 1159 City of London; OS Landranger 176 West London; OS Landranger 177 East London (inn GR 317846).

Canonbury was countryside outside London when the prior and canons of St Bartholomew's in Smithfield had a house here. There are still some surprisingly quiet and grassy areas as this walk proves by following a man-made river to Highbury Fields by way of a church associated with John Betjeman's family.

The Walk

Turn left out of the pub front door and walk up to the road. Go left to enter the late Georgian period Canonbury Square. Walk on the right-hand side where the pavement is built up. Tragedian Thomas Phelps moved into number 8 (marked by a plaque) in 1844 to be near Sadlers Wells Theatre which he was managing. He called it 'an obscure theatre' and his friends thought it could not last a fortnight but he stayed here and ran Sadlers Wells until 1867. At the end go down steps into Canonbury Road, which cuts through the middle of the Square, and cross over to continue through the Square. Evelyn Waugh lived at number 17 in 1928 and ahead is a green plaque next to number 28 to record George Orwell living at 27A in 1945. Turn right to see Canonbury Tower ahead.

Canonbury Tower was a country retreat for the prior and canons of Smithfield's St Bartholomew-the-Great Priory – hence 'canon-bury'. The Chambers of *Chambers Encyclopaedia* fame was a tenant in 1740. Turn right again into Alwyne Villas. After a few yards there is Canonbury Place cul-de-sac where the history of the tower can be found on a garden doorway. The walk continues to the far end of Alwyne Villas to join Canonbury Road and cross the line of the New River. Go left into Canonbury Grove at the side of the Myddleton Arms – named after Sir Hugh Myddleton who masterminded the digging of the New River.

When level with Willow Cottage go left through the gate to join a section of the preserved river although the continuous flow from Hertfordshire now stops at Stoke Newington to the north. Follow the winding path which runs alongside the man-made river dug from Hertford to bring fresh water from the upper reaches of the river Lea in Hertfordshire to the capital. The collection point was near Sadlers Wells, from where water was piped to the City.

Now across the water there are attractive houses and back gardens – one has a tree house. At a road, opposite The Marquess, cross the water to go through a gate on the right. At once the path switches back to the other bank. Stay on the path which at one point crosses a wide inlet on a long wooden bridge.

At a main road cross over to go down Wallace Road opposite. After Canonbury BR station the way ahead becomes the exceptionally wide Petherton Road. Walk on the left-hand side as far as the junction with Leconfield Road but stay in Petherton Road and look for a path on the left between number 107 and Kilteery. Turn left on to the path to walk between a school and a church – St Augustine's, Highbury New Park. Go right to the front of the brick church and cross the road to go up Stradbroke Road opposite. At Balfour Road go right and left into Highbury Grange.

After a short distance go left into Aberdeen Road. This appears to be an ordinary residential street but suddenly there is a fence and a lodge. Here pedestrians can enter Aberdeen Park but note the warning that members of the public do so at their own risk. At a junction go left and follow the road round to the right to find St Saviour's church which features in a John Betjeman poem. The Poet Laureate attended here with his parents but now the building is occupied by the Florence Trust which provides space for artists. Members of the public may try the door.

Further round the bend there is on the left the Foreign Missions Club founded in 1893 and here since 1953. Pass through the gateway at the far end and cross the road to enter Highbury Fields. This is where Wat Tyler gathered his forces during the Peasants Revolt and later it was occupied by thousands made homeless by the Great Fire of London.

After passing the Oasis Café turn left along Church Path – a wide fenced pathway running across the Fields. This path runs into Highbury Place where the houses, built in the 1770s, face the grass. Keep forward, looking for number 25, home of statesman Joseph Chamberlain, and number 1 which was artist Walter Sickert's School of Painting and Engraving from 1927 to 1934.

Cross the main road ahead on the crossing to the post office and turn left. Pass the Highbury & Islington station entrance and the Hedgehog and Hogshead pub. At the florist's shop cross the top of Upper Street using the crossing. Continue ahead for a few yards to go right up steps marked Compton Terrace Garden. Walk ahead along the terrace which dates from about 1800. In the middle of the line of 37 Georgian houses is the Union Chapel opened in 1877 to seat a 1,200 congregation.

At the far end turn left and go left again into Compton Avenue to reach the Compton Arms.

16 Islington
The Narrow Boat

This old canalside pub used to be called the Star but its new name, the Narrow Boat, is appropriate as it is next to the towpath. There are a few seats on the path but the pub entrance is up on the bridge. The front door leads straight into the single bar from where there is a fine view across the water into the entrance of Wenlock Basin. A balcony gives an even better view. The bar extension room is like a barge with a huge photograph of a lock at the far end. Other wall decorations are old maps and views. The furnishing is simple and the floor bare boards.

The menu features Narrow Boat Ploughman's with Stilton or Brie. Also often on the chalk board are lasagne, steaks and a vegetarian dish. This is a Charrington house with Charrington IPA, Draught Bass, Fuller's London Pride and a monthly guest ale.

The Narrow Boat is open 12 noon to 11 pm (10.30 pm Sundays). Food is served 12 noon to 3 pm and 6 pm to 8.30 pm Mondays to Fridays. At weekends there is food only at Sunday lunchtime until 2.30 pm.

Telephone: 0171 226 3906.

How to get there: The Narrow Boat is in Islington at the south end of St Peter's Street, N1 which runs off the south end of the A104 Essex Road. The Angel Underground station is nearby.

Parking: There is very limited on street parking in the area.

Length of the walk: 2¼ miles. Map: A-Z London Street Map; OS Pathfinder 1159 City of London; OS Landranger 176 West London or 177 East London (inn GR 321833).

Starting at the pub by the water, the walk follows the Grand Union Canal to De Beauvoir Town where there is a fine example of Victorian town planning. The return is by way of the parish of St James Prebend Street to pass between the church, shops, pub and

hall of this London village with its historic links to the nearby ancient City of London.

The Walk

Cross the road to go down the steps to the towpath. Turn left to go under the bridge and below the Narrow Boat. There is at once a view to the right down into Wenlock Basin opened in 1826. Now follow the water as far as the fourth bridge, which is round the bend.

First there is Shepherdess Walk Bridge and then across the water a permanently moored café barge before reaching Sturts Lock. Keep on to pass under New North Road followed by the Bridport Place Bridge where Rosemary Works can be seen high up. Just before the narrower tunnel of the next and fourth bridge go up steps on the left where a signpost points to De Beauvoir.

Go ahead to the bridge and turn left along De Beauvoir Road to reach, on the right-hand side, St Peter's church. This is the heart of De Beauvoir Town built in the 1840s and named after landowner Richard de Beauvoir of Guernsey who died in 1708. Behind the church is De Beauvoir Square.

The walk continues opposite the main church door down Northchurch Terrace which leads into Northchurch Road. At the main road (Southgate Road) go ahead up the side of the Dog and Dumpling pub to go left (with the cycle route) into Cleveland Road and then right into Elmore Street. At the Prince Albert pub turn left into Elizabeth Avenue and walk to the far end and New North Road. Here go left along the main road to turn right (by the Texaco garage) into Basire Street. After a short distance turn left with the main traffic into Prebend Street – the name recalls that this area was owned by St Paul's Cathedral which has prebendaries and canons. By the Duchess of Kent pub there is a crossroads with Coleman Fields – built on fields called Great Coleman and Little Coleman.

Soon on the right is St James's church with Victorian almshouses attached at the east end. The Kentish ragstone church was built in 1872 as the successor to the now disappeared St James-in-the-Wall Cripplegate – the site is covered by the Barbican. The new St James's here has medieval glass from the old church. Inside the west door is a bust of William Lambe, Master of the Clothworkers Company, who in 1577 piped fresh water into London – hence Holborn's Lamb's Conduit Street.

Continue ahead to pass the modern St James's Hall on the corner of Packington Street (right). The building was completed in 1994 with the large shell, St James's symbol, being specially made in Greece. The street changes its name to Rheidol Terrace to meet St Peter's Street at a crossroads. Turn left for the Narrow Boat.

17 King's Cross
The Waterside

The Waterside could easily be missed as it looks like part of a modern light industry warehouse or factory. However, inside are the timbers of a real Yorkshire barn which have been used to create an unusually cosy interior and even small rooms. The furnishing is rustic with plenty of horsebrasses. At the back there is another surprise for a terrace overlooks a large stretch of water – hence the name of this new pub. Indeed, the terrace is longer than the pub and runs in front of the next door printing works. The water is the Regent's Canal's Battlebridge Basin and this is often the backdrop for a barbecue.

Across the water today is the London Canal Museum but once the basin was dominated by the wharves of paper manufacturers John Dickinson which received paper from Apsley Mill at Hemel Hempstead and sent the barges, known as 'Paper Mill Dashers' due to their tight schedules, back with wood pulp. The pub site was a brass foundry.

Originally a Hoskins of Leicester pub, this is now a Whitbread house which has introduced a Berni menu. Sandwich varieties

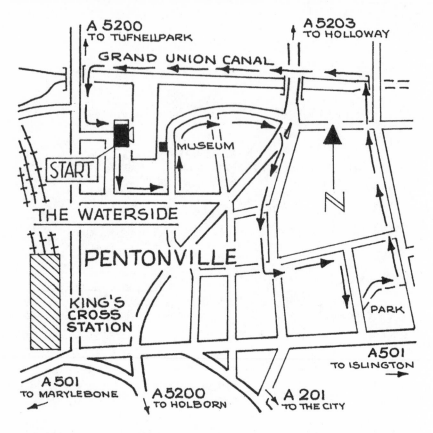

include Cheddar and pickle, prawn and Marie Rose and tuna and mayonnaise. BLT hot baps are a special feature. There is always a soup and main meals include salads, fish and steaks, and two vegetarian dishes. Being a Berni menu there are plenty of puddings such as sherry trifle and ice cream. The pub is popular on Sunday lunchtimes when roast meat is added to the extensive food list. The Waterside Lady narrow boat is sometimes moored here for customers to eat on board. Ales include Whitbread Boddingtons Bitter, Greene King Abbot, Marston's Pedigree and Flowers Original. The times of opening are 11 am to 11 pm weekdays and 12 noon to 10.30 pm on Sundays. Food is served from 12 noon to 2.30 pm and 5.30 pm to 8.30 pm daily.

Telephone: 0171 837 7118.

How to get there: The Waterside, in Crinan Street, N1, has its sign visible from York Way at the side of King's Cross station. The nearest Underground station is King's Cross.

Parking: Limited street spaces evenings and weekends only.

Length of the walk: 1½ miles. Map: A-Z London Street Map; OS Pathfinder 1159 City of London; OS Landranger 176 West London or 177 East London (inn GR 304835).

This walk follows the outside of the canal basin and diverts to the tomb of the first clown before finding the entrance to the long tunnel which takes the canal to east London on its way to join the Thames. The return to the pub is by way of the peaceful towpath.

The Walk

Turn left out of the pub entrance to go south down Crinan Street. At a junction go left into Wharfdale Road. After a few yards there is the entrance to Battlebridge Moorings – the new houses are on the site of a confectionery factory. The walk continues along the road and left into New Wharf Road to pass Gatti's Yard. Beyond Gatti's Wharf is the London Canal Museum housed in the former ice warehouse of Carlo Gatti, the ice cream manufacturer, who established his business here in 1858. Blocks of ice were brought from Norway to London Docks and barged up here for storage in ice wells. The museum is open daily except Mondays.

Continue right along All Saints Street (there used to be a church on the right at the far end) passing Regent's Wharf now occupied by Wolff Olins. At the junction go ahead and right down Calshot Street. After a short distance there is Grimaldi House on the left, marking the site of Joseph Grimaldi's house.

To find the tomb of Grimaldi, the first clown, who died in 1837, turn left into Collier Street and right into Cumming Street. Before the end go left into Joseph Grimaldi Park, formerly St James's churchyard. Keep ahead along the back of the building, which replaced the church, to find Grimaldi's tomb on the right. The replacement building is an underwear factory but the front resembles the church and includes the clown's face at the top. (A painting of the church in 1884 can be found at the Three Hammers in Mill Hill; see Walk 2.)

Continue through the park to Rodney Street and turn left. Keep across a junction by the entrance to Half Moon Crescent. Soon, on the left, there is a view down the canal. The road is above the entrance to a ½ mile long tunnel under Islington. Go through the gate on the left and down to the towpath.

On the far bank there are usually two houseboats moored. Keep forward for a few yards and then turn round to have a view through the tunnel, which opened in 1820. The horses had to be led overground (often by bargees' children) through Chapel Market whilst the rest of the family propelled the barge through the tunnel with their feet. In 1828 a steam tug was introduced and continued in operation for just over a century.

Continue along the towpath to go under Thornhill Bridge which carries Caledonian Road. There is a view of Regent's Wharf before reaching Battlebridge Basin. The Canal Museum is on the left and the Waterside is on the right.

Just before the next bridge (known as Maiden Lane Bridge but now carrying York Way) go up the steps to find a short path leading to the main road. (Only continue under the bridge and ahead for a short distance to see a view of Camley Street Nature Park.) Go left over the canal and left again into Crinan Street to find the Waterside.

18 Wapping
The Captain Kidd

The Captain Kidd on the riverside is a recent addition to Wapping High Street and takes its name from the notorious pirate who was hanged on Wapping waterfront in 1701. The Scottish born New York merchant, who had served as a privateer against the French in the West Indies, was commissioned in 1695 to hunt pirates but instead began to raid vessels in the Indian Ocean. After his arrest he was sent back to England to stand trial. After being hanged at Execution Dock his body was tarred and left to swing from a gibbet downstream at Tilbury as a warning to passing seafarers.

The pub, opened in 1991, is just west of King Henry's Stairs which is the possible site of Execution Dock. The Captain Kidd is largely a new building but maintains the style of a typical warehouse with massive split beams and worn stones. The terrace is at the side which allows the pub windows to open directly above the high tide. The view across the water is of Rotherhithe from where the Pilgrim Fathers sailed in 1620. In the ground floor bar, boards recall the association with the pirate. Shipping prints, some local, decorate the first floor bar. The top floor is the Observation Deck restaurant.

Children are welcome in the upstairs first floor bar where the menu includes the Mobey bap and baguettes with such fillings as Coronation chicken, ham, beef, tuna and cucumber – the huge bap allows for four fillings. The Gallows salad is a blend of four leaves with finely sliced Spanish onions, diced avocado, herbs, croutons and smoked bacon. Soup, jacket potatoes with fillings and Gallows burger are always available, as are coffee, hot chocolate and muffins as the pub is open all day. This is a Samuel Smith house so there are Yorkshire ales including Museum Brew.

The Captain Kidd is open all day from 11.30 am to 11 pm. On Sunday the opening times are 12 noon to 10.30 pm. Food is served from 12 noon until around 10 pm daily and on Sunday there is a roast lunch available as well as the usual menu.

Telephone: 0171 480 5759.

How to get there: The Captain Kidd is almost next door to Wapping police station in the narrow Wapping High Street which can be approached by turning south off The Highway, E1. Nearby in the same street is Wapping Underground station. It is also a short walk from St Katharine Dock next to Tower Bridge.

Parking: No parking available at the pub itself but there is a Pay & Display car park nearby which is free in the evening and all day Sunday.

Length of the walk: 2 miles. Map: A-Z London Street Map; OS Pathfinder 1159 City of London; OS Landranger 177 East London (inn GR 348801).

This walk circles the riverside village of Wapping which until the docks closure could be cut off by raising the lifting bridges on the three approach roads. The route includes the riverside path with its dramatic views and the canalside path which follows the line of the old dockside.

The Walk
Turn right out of the courtyard to follow Wapping High Street past Swan Wharf and King Henry's Stairs. After Gun Wharves there is the end of Wapping Lane to the left. Just past Wapping Underground station go right where the Thames Path is signposted

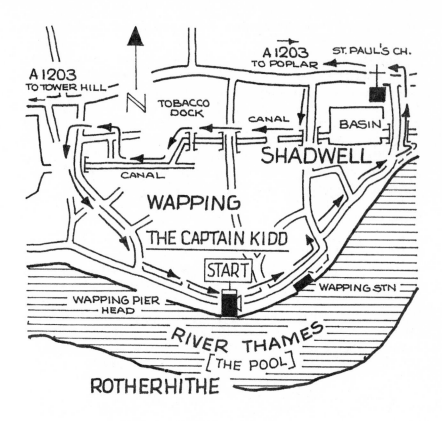

through a narrow gate left unlocked in daylight hours. Go through the passage to find a riverside path running across several residential wharves. There is a view of Canary Wharf tower rising up from the Isle of Dogs behind the land opposite and the much smaller white tower of St Anne's Limehouse on the riverbend.

On returning to the road go ahead past the entrance to New Crane Wharf and a few yards along Garnet Street to turn right into cobbled Wapping Wall, towards the Prospect of Whitby. The pub was built in 1520 but adopted its present name in 1777 after a ship called the *Prospect*, registered in Whitby, was moored outside for so long that it became a landmark. It was here that a sailor sold a plant from the West Indies and so introduced the fuchsia to the British Isles.

Beyond the pub do not go left with the road but ahead into Prospect Wharf and bear right for the riverside path. Follow the winding way round to the old entrance to Shadwell basin. Once back at the road, Glamis Road, cross the lifting bridge and walk up to The Highway main road. Ahead is a fine view of St Mary's Cable Street – the church is famous for its Catholic Anglican tradition and the street for the 1936 Battle of Cable Street when East Enders blocked the route of a Mosleyite march.

Go left along The Highway to pass St Paul's Shadwell, known as 'The Sea Captains' church'. Captain James Cook was an active parishioner and his son was baptised here in 1763 – just 13 years after President Jefferson's mother, Jane. St Paul's was rebuilt in 1820. Continue along the road to go left down Garnet Street to reach a lifting bridge. Just before the bridge go right down a zig-zag slope to reach the canal. Turn away from the bridge and where the water ends continue across the park to find the water reappearing. Keep the canal on the left to walk under Wapping Lane and pass the pirate ships moored in dry dock outside Tobacco Dock.

After a pedestrian swingbridge the water turns south-west – although once the bridge marked the end of a small dock and the entrance to the vast Western Dock water. At a junction of water the bust of Docks engineer John Rennie can be seen looking down opposite. Turn right with the canalside path to walk to the far end of the promenade. Across the water is the old southern side of the Western Dock. Do not go under the bridge (the old exit to the Thames) at the bend but turn right to walk through Waveney Close.

At the street go left along Kennet Street and left again at a junction to cross the water. Stay on this road, Vaughan Way, and just past Codling Close bear right with the main traffic into Sampson Street to reach Wapping High Street. Opposite is Black Eagle Wharf. Go left along the cloister by the road and past Wapping Pierhead. This is the original entrance to London Docks dug in 1805 with the houses for officials added in 1811-13. The garden replaced the water after the docks closed in 1969. The Town of Ramsgate at Wapping Old Stairs is named after Ramsgate fishermen who landed catches here. Oliver's Wharf next door was the first docklands warehouse conversion to flats in 1970. In Scandrett Street is the restored St John's school dating from 1795.

Continue ahead along Wapping High Street to pass the police launch depot and, after Wapping New Stairs, Wapping River police station dating from 1798. Just beyond is the Captain Kidd.

19 Bulls Cross
The Pied Bull

The Pied Bull stands on the Ermine Street Roman road and dates from the 16th century but it has been a pub only since 1790. It was first a stables and kennels which is why at the front the ceiling is so low – indeed, one beam is wrapped in padding to save customers' heads!

More recently it was the childhood home of prolific garden writer Frances Perry (1907-1993) who spent most her life in the village, inspired by E.A. Bowles, gardener at nearby Myddleton House, she helped to found Capel Manor garden research centre. She died at her desk in Bulls Cross Cottage a few yards to the south of the Pied Bull.

Food is served at the back of the pub near the conservatory, where children are welcome. The ploughman's choice includes cider roast ham and there are also sandwiches and rolls, with pasta or fish for main dishes. Cider roast ham is also served with a fried egg, salad and chips. The burgers include a Plain Jane and the Pied Bull burger which is beef with two rashers of bacon and cheese. Specials can include pancakes and on Sunday there is a roast. This is

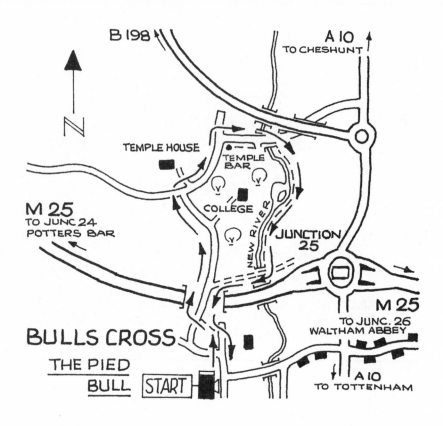

a Whitbread house serving Boddingtons Bitter, Marston's Pedigree and Flowers Original.

The opening hours are 11 am to 11 pm with food available 12 noon to 9 pm except Saturday afternoon when only drinks are served between 3 pm and 7 pm. The Sunday hours are 12 noon to 10.30 pm with food available until 3 pm and after 7.30 pm to 10 pm.

Telephone: 01992 710619.

How to get there: The Pied Bull is at Bulls Cross opposite the western end of Bullsmoor Lane off the A10 Cambridge Road, north of Enfield. Turkey Street BR station is nearby.

Parking: The pub's own car park to the side of the building.

Length of the walk: 3 miles. Map: A-Z Master Atlas of Greater London; OS Pathfinder 1140 Barnet & Enfield and 1120 Hatfield & Cheshunt; OS Landranger 166 Luton & Hertford (inn GR 343996).

It is sometimes hard to believe that Bulls Cross is in London. Even if it is left off many street maps this area is part of the London Borough of Enfield. However, this walk does cross the M25 and Greater London boundary and for a very good reason. Hidden in the trees on a brewer's estate is a famous building from the City of London. The return route is by way of a path by the New River, dug to bring clean water to the City.

The Walk

Turn left out of the pub entrance to walk past the junction with Bullsmoor Lane. On the left are Myddleton Cottages – named after the founder of the New River. Beyond the cottages is The Orchards. At the bend in the road cross over with care to continue ahead down Gilmour Close. This junction was a crossroads until Bullsmoor Lane was moved a few yards south to create privacy for the early 18th-century Capel Manor which can be seen through the fence on the right. The north-south road is the former Ermine Street built by the Romans to link London and Lincoln.

Squeeze past the car barrier across the road and walk down the road. Cross the stile by the lodge built when this was the entrance to Theobalds Park. Through the fence on the left can be seen part of Capel Manor's 30 acre garden which includes the *Gardening Which*? trials garden (entrance in Bullsmoor Lane).

The drive ahead is now cut off by the M25 so bear left to go over a stile and across a field to a second stile. Climb the bank to a road, Bullscross Ride, and turn right to go over the M25. At the end of the bridge you pass out of Greater London and into Hertfordshire. Continue ahead and stay on the right-hand side of the road when the pavement ends. To the left there is a Jewish cemetery and later a Caravan Club site to the right. On approaching the huge gateway to Theobalds Park bear left with the road.

The road curves round the park to a T-junction at Temple House. Here go right along Old Park Ride to pass Gardener's Cottage. Keep forward beyond a barrier. The road runs gently downhill to a

Temple Bar, once an entrance to the City of London – now in rural Hertfordshire.

junction. Turn right to find Temple Bar on the right.

Temple Bar, maybe designed by Christopher Wren, was the entrance to the City of London at the east end of The Strand from 1670 to 1877 when the archway was found to be too narrow for the increasing traffic. After a decade of storage the stones were brought here to be the entrance to brewer Sir Henry Bruce Meux's Theobalds Park estate. His Horseshoe Brewery was in Tottenham Court Road on the site of The Dominion and it was his wife, a former barmaid at the Horseshoe tavern, who was the driving force for bringing the gateway here. In its early days in central London the heads of executed prisoners were displayed on the top.

Continue past Temple Bar on the woodland path, known as Theobalds Lane, which after ¼ mile passes the entrance to the Tesco staff playing field just before crossing the New River. Somewhere near here James I fell off his horse into the newly dug river when inspecting work. However, the king was an enthusiastic supporter of the scheme and Myddleton was knighted soon afterwards.

At once go right through a kissing-gate to follow the path along the river bank. Across the water there are views of Theobalds Park mansion which is now a college. To the left can be seen the square tower of Waltham Abbey 2 miles away. Beyond is Epping Forest. Ahead early on can be seen the Canary Wharf tower on the Isle of Dogs 13 miles to the south.

The path bends as the water widens by a rare island in the river. On eventually reaching a bridge cross the water to follow a narrow enclosed path running between woodland and a field. On reaching the old Theobalds Park drive (cut off by the M25) go ahead up the steps to the new road. Turn left to cross the M25 and on the far side look out for the way down to the stile. Cross the field to a second stile and go right past the lodge and walk back to the Pied Bull.

20 Lea Bridge
The Prince of Wales

On the west side of Lea Bridge the road is flanked by two pub signs – the Ship in Distress and the Prince of Wales. The latter is on the river Lea towpath with a view of the weir from both the main bar and the terrace where most people eat in summer. This is the first waterside pub and often the first stop for walkers on the 50 mile Lea Valley Path which follows the navigation from Three Mills in the south to Leagrave just north of Luton. There has been a road crossing here at Lea Bridge since at least 1745 and a Prince of Wales pub since the 1860s.

The inn's partly panelled walls are decorated with pictures of past Princes of Wales such as Charles II and Edward VII, as well as Prince Charles. There is also a large colour photograph of his grandmother, the Queen Mother, pulling a pint of Young's Special Bitter in a Stepney pub. The chairs are well upholstered and there are window seats. Although children are welcome the rule here is that they should be at least 14 years of age.

The food is a major attraction with six versions of a ploughman's including tuna; 'mixed five bean' heads the salad list and jacket potatoes come topped with cheese, baked beans, tuna or vegetable chilli. There are always four vegetarian dishes available. The brunch choices include jumbo sausage and chips. Spotted dick is always on the pudding list. On Sundays roast beef lunch is also on offer. Being a Young's house there is real ale and such favourites as Young's Bitter, Special and Winter Warmer.

The Prince of Wales is open 11 am to 11 pm with food available 12 noon to 3 pm and 6 pm to 9.30 pm. The Sunday opening hours are 12 noon to 10.30 pm with food available until 2.30 pm.

Telephone: 0181 533 3463.

How to get there: Lea Bridge is on the A104 just east of Clapton and towards the west end of Lea Bridge Road, E5. The nearest

The canal towpath at Hackney Marsh.

stations (BR) are Clapton and Lea Bridge. Buses 38, 48, 56 cross the bridge and pass the pub.

Parking: There is a public car park next door to the pub.

Length of the walk: 2½ miles. Map: A-Z London Street Map; OS Pathfinder 1159 City of London; OS Landranger 177 East London (inn GR 356866).

Lea Bridge is a crossing on the river Lea which flows south from Hertford to form an important boundary. It was the London county boundary with Essex and remains that of the Diocese of London – the east bank is in the Chelmsford diocese. Today the river here is the divide between the London boroughs of Hackney and Waltham Forest. This walk explores Hackney Marsh which today is bounded by the old river Lea and the 'new' river Lea navigation.

The Walk
Leave the pub by the terrace door and walk ahead downstream on the towpath – and not under Lea Bridge. Across the water is the weir and the course of the old river Lea. There is a handy information board at the beginning of the navigation channel dug in the 1770s and at first known as the Hackney Cut. There is a bridge over an inlet just before the weir keeper's cottage alongside an entrance to Mill Fields. The name recalls Lea Bridge Mill which was built at the junction of the new and old river Lea across the water. Notice the old LCC boundary markers at the Fields entrance.

Walk past the cottage and follow the towpath over the canal's former floodgates to walk alongside the long wall of the Middlesex Filter Beds, built in 1852 to supply clean water to London, which since being abandoned in 1969 have become a nature reserve. The gateway is open for visitors at least from 10 am to 4 pm and later at summer weekends. As many as 14 different species of butterflies can be seen here. On either side of the wall there might be moorhens, mallards, cormorants and herons. When the wall ends bear left through a squeeze stile to leave the water. A short path runs to a T-junction with a metalled approach to the filter beds. Continue ahead over the grass and another path towards the line of trees half left. To the right can be seen Canary Wharf tower on the Isle of Dogs 4 miles to the south.

The poplars mark the winding route of the original river Lea. Alongside the river there is a track which should be followed as far as the river's bend to the south. Here there is the first clear view of the river. Leave the main path to follow the parallel grass path nearer the water. Here, with no craft, there are reeds growing in the water and often plenty of Canada geese as well as swans and herons. Later there is a view of the modern Spitalfields fruit market built on the former Temple Mills railway marshalling yard.

The river bends again to reach a bridge. There was once a ferry here and, on the far side, the White House pub frequented by highwayman Dick Turpin. Do not cross the bridge. Turn right to walk across the vast expanse of grass. Cattle were run on these 337 acres until 1893. Half left ahead by the canal is the Lesney factory where metal for the famous Matchbox toys arrived by barge.

On reaching the canal turn right to walk upstream. Soon there is a gap in the fence to allow walkers to join the parallel towpath. Brick Lock was just past the bend. The second bridge has been known as Cow Bridge since the early 19th century. Millfields Road on the far side leading down from Clapton Pond was known as Marsh Lane when it ran directly on to the marsh. After the canal cut was built the road became Pound Lane and later Pond Lane. In summer the land near the bridge is often a camp site.

On reaching the filter beds wall the towpath joins the outward route. Keep ahead to return to the Prince of Wales.